CW01551648

# 75 WOF
# LAWYERS USE
# DIFFERENTLY

# 75 WORDS THAT LAWYERS USE DIFFERENTLY

## COMMON WORDS USED IN UNCOMMON WAYS

## GRAHAM GOVER LLB, SOLICITOR
### SECOND LANGUAGE LEGAL ENGLISH

## DEDICATION

This book is dedicated to Kohei and Eriko,
two lawyers who put me on the path
to teach legal English.

# CONTENTS

# INTRODUCTION

It is often said that lawyers speak a different language to everyone else.

All professionals use jargon - special words or expressions that are difficult for those outside their circle to understand - but lawyers use words in different, and sometimes in opposite, ways to how they are popularly understood. Or, as the subtitle of this book puts it, they use common words in uncommon ways.

This book was written for lawyers and law students who need to improve their English language skills to practice law in English as a second (or third or fourth) language.

You may well be familiar with how the words *fee*, *find* and *friend* are used in everyday English, but what do lawyers mean when they use them? Or *serve*, *suit* and *stay*? Or *call*, *cause* and *caution*?

Here you will find 75 such words that I have drawn from four decades of legal practice in England, and my experience as a teacher of English as a second language to other lawyers. There are many more, and I have excluded some of the more common ones that you may have already read in other legal English books (*consideration*, for example) but you have to stop somewhere.

I hope this book will be of value to you as you seek to gain a greater knowledge of English so that you can practice law internationally.

Graham Gover, LLB Solicitor
slle.uk
July 2024

# HOW TO USE THIS BOOK

The purpose of this book is to introduce you to the idea that lawyers use common words in uncommon ways. I have identified 75 such words, and I have set out the difference between the word's most common meaning and the way it is used by lawyers.

For example, for Word #1 action, I have written:

## ITS MOST COMMON MEANING:
1. The state or process of doing something or being active.

## ITS USE BY LAWYERS:
6. A civil case brought by one party against another, seeking remedy of a wrong or recovery of what is due.

Each definition is given a number, and in this book, its most common meaning is always number 1 because it is the first meaning given to the word by the dictionary's editors.

Some dictionaries order words with multiple meanings by placing the oldest use first, but I have used those that order words by frequency of use first.

The word order given throughout this book is taken from Collins English Dictionary, Thirteenth Edition 2018. The Dictionary's introductory Guide states:

> *Order of senses*
>
> *As a general rule, where a headword has more than one sense, the first sense given is the one most common in current usage ... Subsequent senses are arranged so as to give a coherent account of the meaning of a headword ... Technical senses usually follow general senses.*

The Dictionary also notes where the word has a legal usage, by placing the word *law* after the order number.

By adopting their definitions and technical (legal) uses, I have been able to show how one word has both a common meaning and a technical (legal) meaning, and the numbers indicate just how different in meaning they are.

If no number is given against the lawyer's use of the word, the symbol (-) appears, which means that the dictionary has not listed that meaning. We cannot expect a general language dictionary to list the legal meaning of a particular word. I have used my own experience as a lawyer to know that it has a different legal meaning. I have also confirmed this by consulting both English and American legal dictionaries.

The entry for each of the 75 words is laid out in this way:

1.  The word (the symbol # here means *number*, rather than *hashtag*);

2.  The type of word such as noun, verb or adjective;

3.  The category of word, which I have divided into general law, court procedure, land and property, lawyers, criminal law, and contracts;

4.  Its most common meaning;

5.  Its use by lawyers;

6.  An explanation of its use in common speech;

7.  An explanation of how lawyers use that word differently, with associated words and phrases and an introduction to its wider legal use. If a word appears in the text that is one of the 75 words, its # number is given;

8. A summary of the difference in meaning and use; and

9. A list of other entries in which that word is used, giving you yet more associated words and phrases.

The order in which the words have been presented, from #1 to #75, also follows the frequency in which they are used in the English language, with *action* being the most common and *recital* being the least. This word frequency order is taken from the one billion word Corpus of Contemporary American English (COCA; www.english-corpora.org/coca), the only corpus of English that is large, up-to-date, and based on a wide range of genres.

The words have also been listed at the end of this book in alphabetical order and separately by category.

I have attempted to mark the difference in legal usage between British and American English. As a lawyer with forty years of experience in legal practice in English, I am most familiar with that jurisdiction, so I naturally tend to refer to it more frequently.

I have also attempted to write a book about language rather than law, so the usual disclaimer applies. Please do not rely on anything in this book as legal advice on which to base actions.

So after all that, here are the 75 words.

# WORD #1: ACTION
## Type: noun    Category: court procedure

## ITS MOST COMMON MEANING:
1. The state or process of doing something or being active.

## ITS USE BY LAWYERS:
6. A civil case brought by one party against another, seeking remedy of a wrong or recovery of what is due.

> *The film was pure action from start to finish.*
>
> *John was always a man of action. He could never sit still for long.*
>
> *This emergency requires immediate action if we are to prevent a crisis.*
>
> *Most of the play's action takes place in a bar.*
>
> *She has so much energy, she always wants to be where the action is.*

To most people, *action* is dynamic, fast-paced, and energetic. As always, lawyers are never this exciting in real life. To lawyers, an action is a case (see #14) that is started in the civil courts where one party sues another for a wrong done, to protect a right, or to prevent a wrong. Sometimes, action is used for criminal cases, too.

## USE OF *ACTION* AND WORDS ASSOCIATED WITH IT
Lawyers **bring an action**.

> *Carswells brought an **action for libel** against the Newspaper Group plc.*

This was a **libel action**, the cause of action being an article about the private life of one of Carswells' clients that their client claimed was deliberately false. He had a right of action because he was the person whose reputation was harmed. He was advised by counsel (#53) that the article was actionable—there was sufficient evidence, and the libel laws of the UK supported the claim—but the chance of success was fifty-fifty.

Lawyers also say *an action **in** trespass*, or *actionable **in** tort,* to identify the particular law that applies to the case.

> *I was advised that the case is actionable **in** tort rather than **in** contract.*

But watch out for *an action **at** common law.*

An action **for** possession, **for** divorce, or **for** damages identifies the intended outcome of the action or the reason for bringing the action.

There are always parties **to** the action: for example, a claimant and a defendant. The defendant pursues their defence **to** the action brought against them.

If the parties agree that the case does not need to be continued, there can be a **settlement of the action,** and the parties can sign a consent order agreeing to the outcome of the action. There can also be a **discontinuance of action**, so that a claimant may discontinue all or part of a claim at any time by filing a notice of discontinuance with the court and serving copies on the other parties.

Pre-action protocols, introduced in the UK in 1999, speed up the early parts of the litigation process before the action is started. They encourage greater contact between the parties at the earliest possible opportunity to narrow the issues (#34) and encourage better and earlier information exchange for fair and early settlement of claims.

A **class action** is a lawsuit started by one or more parties on behalf not only of themselves but also of many other parties, when common questions of law and fact are involved, for example where the use of a drug caused identical harm to each claimant.

## SUMMARY

*Action* typically means the effort of doing something, usually to achieve a defined purpose. To a lawyer, an action is just one type of effort; a court case.

## OTHER ENTRIES THAT USE THE WORD *ACTION*

#3 real, #4 stay, #14 case, #17 cause, #18 matter, #31 suit, #42 proceed.

# WORD #2: FRIEND

## Type: noun    Category: court procedure

**ITS MOST COMMON MEANING:**

1. Someone who is not a family member who you know well and like a lot.

**ITS USE BY LAWYERS:**

(-) How one lawyer refers to another when speaking to the judge in court.

The everyday meaning of *friend* is very well known. Who do you think of when I ask who was your best friend at school; what did you enjoy doing with them, and why did you like them the most?

Then, picture two lawyers in court, arguing strongly for their clients, raising objections to questions put to the witness, opposing every argument and trying to destroy their opponent's case. That can appear at times to be the opposite of friendly behaviour: they seem to be enemies, trying their best to win and for the other to lose! And yet, when one lawyer speaks to the judge they call the other lawyer their friend.

> *Your honour, I served a copy of this new statement on those instructing my learned friend more than four weeks ago.*
>
> *With respect, your honour, none of the points made by my learned friend are in any way convincing.*

Did you spot the word *learned* in these quotations? In this context, it has two syllables and is pronounced *lern-ed*, not *lernd.* When the person being referred to is a barrister, they are "my learned friend", and other lawyers (like me!) are just "my friend". *Learned* here means someone who has acquired much knowledge and understanding from careful study but is reserved exclusively for barristers.

Lawyers don't call each other *friend*; they only refer to the lawyer as *friend* when speaking to the judge. It is used as a mark of respect and courtesy from one lawyer to another, but it still doesn't explain why the word *friend* is used. American lawyers don't use this word and refer to each other as *counsel*, or *counselor* when speaking directly.

## SUMMARY

In life, a friend is someone you like and for whom you would happily do anything. In court, lawyers can be tough, even aggressive, opponents and fight hard for their clients. Their behaviour can seem anything but friendly, but courtesy requires them to refer to their opponent as their friend.

# WORD #3: REAL

## Type: adjective    Category: land and property

## ITS MOST COMMON MEANING:
1. Existing or occurring in the physical world; not imaginary, fictitious, or theoretical; actual.

## ITS USE BY LAWYERS
8. Land and buildings.

The laptop that I am using to write this book is real. My fingers are typing out the words I can see on a real screen. I took it out of a real bag and placed it on a real table, on which is also a real cup of coffee and a real plate of biscuits. All of these items are real and they are my property. A lawyer would agree that this is indeed property, but a lawyer would not say that this is **real property**.

For property to be *real* it has to be land and buildings, fixed and immovable. We are familiar with the term **real estate** (the land and property that a person owns), which US lawyers call **realty**. In the US a person who buys and sells real estate is a **realtor**. An action (#1) to recover **real property** is called a **real action**.

Anything that is not fixed and is movable is what a lawyer calls *personal property*.

## SUMMARY
My laptop is real in the everyday sense, but it is not real property in the legal sense. For real.

## OTHER ENTRIES THAT USE THE WORD *REAL*
#36 fee

# WORD #4: STAY

## Type: verb    Category: court procedure

## ITS MOST COMMON MEANING:

1. To continue or remain in a certain place, state or position.

## ITS USE BY LAWYERS:

20. To suspend or stop a court case or judgment of the court.

We use the word *stay* to talk about something that continues as it is or remains the same.

> *I came for one day; I stayed for six months.*
>
> *"San Diego, stay classy!" said Ron Burgundy in the film Anchorman.*
>
> *I decided from an early age to stay away from drugs.*
>
> *Put the food in the freezer so it stays edible for a long time.*
>
> *For the last five years, I have been a stay-at-home mum.*

Lawyers use *stay* to mean *to stop* something and not continue, whether for a short time or even permanently. A **stay of proceedings** imposes a halt on the current action. Courts have the power to stay the whole or any part of a case; to **stay a case** either permanently or for a short time; and to stay a case until an event happens such as the outcome of an appeal or application.

Sometimes a court case has ended and the judge orders the enforcement of its decision. Imagine a case in which a defendant has been convicted of murder and the court imposes the death penalty. If new evidence is discovered that could reverse the guilty verdict, their attorney might request a **stay of execution** (see #50). This would halt the execution process, allowing time for the new evidence to be fully examined and considered by the court. Or, if a President issued a pardon, there would be an automatic and permanent stay of execution.

If a temporary stay is ended and the case restarts, it is called **a lifting of the stay**.

## SUMMARY

*Stay* is one of those words which lawyers use in a way that is opposite to its general meaning. They use it to mean stop, whereas in everyday use it means to continue.

# WORD #5: FIND
Type: verb    Category: court procedure

## ITS MOST COMMON MEANING:
1. To discover, either unexpectedly or after careful searching.

## ITS USE BY LAWYERS:
6. To decide a court case, tribunal or inquiry.

> *You will find the knives in the top drawer.*
>
> *The child was found safe and well after he had been missing for twelve hours.*
>
> *Finally, I found somewhere close to college to live.*
>
> *I've just found a $10 note in my jacket pocket.*

Some things are found by accident (like the $10 note) or after years of study (like finding a cure for a disease).

Lawyers use the word *find* to mean *making a determination or a decision* after hearing evidence or legal argument. For example in a jury trial, it is said that the jury **found** the defendant guilty. When the court asks the jury foreman about the decision, they are asked this question:

> *On count 1 of the indictment, do you find the defendant guilty or not guilty?*

We say that a person is convicted of an offence either if they plead guilty or are **found guilty** after a trial.

After a legal argument in a case, you might hear a judge say

| *I find for the defence*

meaning, I agree with the argument put forward by defence counsel (see #53). That is also called the **judge's finding,** just as a conviction by a jury is a **guilty finding** or a **finding of guilt.**

In a civil case, a defendant can be **found liable in negligence** or **found liable for (to pay) damages.**

We sometimes refer to a court's decision as a **finding of fact**, such as the fact that the defendant was at home at the time of the assault that took place in a bar and, therefore, could not be found guilty of that assault. In a jury trial, the jurors are the **finders of fact**, and the judge then guides the jury on the relevant law to apply to the **facts they have found**.

In the magistrates' court, the chair of the bench can be heard to say

| *We find the case proved (or not proved)*

## SUMMARY
Sometimes a thing can be found by accident, but in law a finding is a decision made after careful thought and consideration.

# WORD #6: CALL

Type: noun    Category: lawyers

## ITS MOST COMMON MEANING:
1. To speak or utter (words, sounds, etc) loudly to attract attention.

## ITS USE BY LAWYERS:
24. A measure of seniority of a lawyer.

The word *call* (as a noun) has found its way into general conversation in many ways. As well as a *phone call,* there is a visit (*I paid a call to my good friend Jim*), a travel stop (*the train makes three calls before arriving in London*), a decision (*that was a good call!*), the sound of a bird (*the strange call of a swift)* and the right to decide (*it's your call about where we have lunch*).

Lawyers have different levels of experience and seniority. Some cases require a lawyer who has gained experience from conducting the same kind of case again and again, which requires time in which to acquire the necessary skills to succeed. As a solicitor, it is sometimes necessary to instruct counsel (a barrister, see #53), and when speaking with their clerk I ask about their *call*, that is for how long they have practised at the bar (#23). "She has twenty years' call". This is a shorthand way of saying *it's twenty years since she was called to the bar*, and that is one way to measure counsel's expertise as a lawyer.

The **call date** is when barristers are formally recognised to have passed the vocational stage of training and have been called (#23) to the Bar by their Inn of Court (#63).

Barristers are often referred to by the year of their **year of call,** which is calculated from the same date.

## SUMMARY
In general, in English, a call is very short, but a lawyer's call is measured in years.

## OTHER ENTRIES THAT USE THE WORD *CALL*
#23 bar, #63 inns

# WORD #7: HEAR

## Type: verb　　Category: court procedure

**ITS MOST COMMON MEANING:**
1. To receive or become aware of sound using your ears. The act of receiving sound.

**ITS USE BY LAWYERS:**
5. To decide a case in a court.

We can hear without making any effort. Sound comes at us from all directions and many sources. We are born with the ability to hear; sadly, our hearing fails as we age.

Lawyers use the word *hear* about a case (see #14) in which a judge makes a formal and binding decision after hearing from all parties, their evidence and submissions. That's why a case is also called a *hearing*.

Did you notice the words *hearing from* in the earlier sentence? The judge *hears* the case both in the sense of hearing what the parties have to say, and *hears* in the sense of trying the issues and making a formal, legal determination. To *hear* means to listen to the lawyers and witnesses with attention, and to *hear* also means to make a judicial inquiry into and a decision on the facts.

**SUMMARY**
In daily life, we hear all the time because sound is everywhere, but a case is heard when there has been a formal decision by a judge after reviewing the evidence and the law.

## OTHER ENTRIES THAT USE THE WORD *HEAR*
#26 audience

# WORD #8: HOLD

### Type: verb    Category: court procedure

## ITS MOST COMMON MEANING:

1. To grasp with or keep in your hand.

## ITS USE BY LAWYERS:

(-) In the case of a judge, to make a binding decision having heard the facts, evidence and submissions of the parties.

In general English, a hand is used to hold something. Lovers hold hands. I held a pen when editing the paper draft of this book. In my wedding vows, I promised "to have and to hold" my spouse, meaning to keep close and care for her. I have *held on to* my wedding suit, too: it still fits. The idea here is to hold, to grasp, to keep safe.

Some beliefs can also be firmly held. Take for instance the Declaration of Independence by which the United States Congress on July 4, 1776 declared:

> *We **hold** these truths to be self-evident, that all men are created equal, that they are endowed by their Creator with certain unalienable Rights, that among these are Life, Liberty and the pursuit of Happiness.*

This is a figurative (non-literal) meaning of the word *hold*.

Lawyers use the word *hold* in yet another way.

> *This ground has been largely overtaken by my conclusion that the Inspector erred in law in his approach to the decision-making process. However, **I have held** that the*

> *Inspector's reasons were inadequate at paragraphs 32 and 42 of my judgment.*

> *As **the Deputy Judge held** in the Surrey Homes case, even the issue of "not materially larger" does not always depend simply on a floor space comparison but must also be judged by reference to other factors which might affect openness.*

> *On the application:*

> ***Held, granting the application**, (1) that the question whether a development plan was "absent" for the purposes of paragraph 14 of the NPPF was a question of fact;*

These quotations are from case reports in which a judge **has held**, meaning the judge has made a formal decision that they were asked to make in the case before them. To *hold* means to decide. Whenever you read the word *hold* or *held* about a court case, the word *decide* and *decided* can be used in its place without any loss of meaning or accuracy.

See also #5 find.

## SUMMARY
We hold things with our hands, but judges hold them with their minds: they decide (or hold) after hearing each side's case.

# WORD #9: PERSON
## Type: noun     Category: general law

## ITS MOST COMMON MEANING:
1. An individual human being.

## ITS USE BY LAWYERS:
4. A human person or a corporation or other entity with its own legal identity.

Non-native speakers of English easily understand the word *person*. A person is an individual human being; a man, woman or child.

> *The price of admission is $10 per person*
>
> *The person who invented the internet is a genius*
>
> *Every person on this planet deserves to live a happy and healthy life.*

It can be used to describe or characterise someone.

> *I'm not a morning person (or a cat person, or an outdoor person, or a coffee person).*

meaning they don't like mornings, cats, the outdoors, or coffee.

In contrast, the law can recognise humans and non-humans as a person. In law, there are *natural persons* (see #21) and *legal persons*. You will understand *natural persons* from what I have written here: they are individual human beings. A *legal person* is a collection of individual humans who make up an entity which is separate and distinct from those humans. The best example of that is a corporation, which has directors, managers and other employees. A corporation (for example, Ford Motor Company Limited) is a person who is different from any of its directors, managers, and employees. A corporation is a person that can enter into contracts and own land in its name and on its own account.

A corporation may also commit a criminal offence as it is still a person, although there are practical limitations. A corporation cannot drive a car carelessly or start a fight. Courts have had to decide if a statute that refers to a person applies equally to a natural and a legal person, for example, whether a corporation was a person who could attend court to give evidence, or was a person who could hold an auctioneer's licence (it couldn't in both cases).

## SOME WORDS, PHRASES AND USES OF *PERSON*

*Person* is gender neutral and is therefore helpful to avoid using male-centred words. You can use *chairperson* in place of *chairman*.

If a party to court proceedings (see #42) appears without a lawyer, they are said to **appear in person**.

**Personal property** is all property other than land, buildings and interests in land (#3).

Some documents require **personal service** (#13).

A will requires executors and administrators to distribute the property left in a will (#62). Together, they are known as **personal representatives**.

## IS IT *PERSONS* OR *PEOPLE*?

In everyday speech, the plural of person is *people*, but in formal and legal writing, the word *persons* is often used. In the first example given above,

> *The price of admission is $10 per person*

you could continue

> *so that would be $40 for four people*

but not *that would be $40 for four persons.*

But lawyers do use the word persons in formal documents. The UK has a statute called the Children and Young Persons Act 2008. It's not the Children and Young People Act. That style of drafting continues within statutes themselves. The focus is on each person as an individual, even though they may form a larger group of people (all young persons).

> *(7) A collecting authority may withdraw a liability notice issued by it by giving notice to that effect in writing to the persons on whom it was served.*

Here, a single notice is not served on a group as a whole, but separate notices are served on individual persons.

That's also why we refer to *persons of interest* (individuals, each of whom is a suspect in a crime) and why the sign reads:

> *Any person or persons damaging this building will be prosecuted*

The law respects the individual, be they young persons or disabled persons, and imposes duties on all persons. It is essential, therefore, if you are drafting a formal document in English to recognise the significance of the word *persons*. When writing informally, you would use *people*, but in formal writing, where the focus is on individuals within a group, you would use *persons* to refer to that group.

## SUMMARY

Generally, a person is a human being, but in law, a non-human being may also be a person.

## OTHER ENTRIES THAT USE THE WORD *PERSON*

#21 natural

# WORD #10: PROVIDE

## Type: verb    Category: contracts

## ITS MOST COMMON MEANING:

1. To give what is needed.

## ITS USE BY LAWYERS:

5. To require that something must happen.

The word *provide* has an easily understood meaning in everyday English. In this sense as a verb, it means to give, supply or make available.

> *The government provides free health care for people over 60.*
>
> *He provided free uniforms for each member of the soccer team.*
>
> *Curtains provide privacy to occupiers of the house.*

In its legal sense, the verb *provide* is used to make a requirement or state that something will or must happen.

> *The US Constitution **provides** that its state legislature has two bodies: the House of Representatives and the Senate.*
>
> *Your lease **provides** that 28 days' notice must be given if you wish to give up occupation of the building.*
>
> *The case of Dobbs v. Jackson Women's Health Organization (2022) **provides** that there is no constitutional right to an abortion.*

> *Section 1 of the Theft Act 1968* **provides** *that there must be an element of dishonesty for stealing to be a criminal offence.*

> *Your employment contract at clause 5.1* **provides** *that all the work you produce as an employee belongs to the company that employs you.*

The item referred to in each example above is a definitive statement, a binding authority, or something that must be acknowledged and complied with and has legal force, whether found in a statute, a leading case, a contract, or a constitution. It *provides* in the sense that compliance is required.

The present continuous tense (*provides*) is used because it continues to be binding for as long as the statute is in force, or the case has not been overturned. If the statute is repealed, or the case is overturned, or the contract comes to an end, we would use the past tense:

> *The case of Roe v Wade (1973)* **provided** *that there was a constitutional right to an abortion until it was overturned in 2022 by the case of Dobbs.*

## SUMMARY

The word *provide* commonly means something that is given, often freely and that meets a need. Lawyers use it when something is to be done.

## OTHER ENTRIES THAT USE THE WORD *PROVIDE*

#13 service

# WORD #11: INFORMATION

Type: noun    Category: court procedure

## ITS MOST COMMON MEANING:
1. News, facts or knowledge.

## ITS USE BY LAWYERS:
5. The document that starts criminal proceedings.

We live in the information age. The entire world of knowledge - the information superhighway - is available with the tap of a smartphone screen.

However, in both the US and the UK, an information is a document that commences criminal proceedings, but the procedures are very different in each jurisdiction.

In England and Wales, a person can be brought before the criminal courts in two ways: arrest and charge (or arrest, charge and then bailed to appear at court) or by summons. To obtain a summons, the prosecutor must **lay an information** before the magistrates' court which must inform the accused, in clear and unambiguous language, of the alleged offence so that they can consider how they intend to plead, or start preparing their defence or mitigation. The details of the information are copied onto the summons which is then served on the accused.

In the US, an information also arises in criminal cases. The US Constitution affords its citizens the right to have their cases assessed by a grand jury. That right can be waived (for example because the accused intends to plead guilty or to plea bargain) and instead of a grand jury indictment, the criminal process is started by **filing an information**.

## SUMMARY

In the real world, *information* is a collection of facts on a given subject. In the legal world, *an information* is a document that alleges a criminal offence.

***Please also note*** that in its common meaning, *information* is an uncountable noun. You would not say. "We have many informations about the paintings in this exhibition". Instead, you would say "We have much information" or "a lot of information". In the legal world, there can be many informations, because each information is a separate allegation, or many people can be the subject of separate informations.

*The State laid ten informations alleging assault, one for each member of the group that was involved in the fight.*

# WORD #12: TAXATION

## Type: noun    Category: court procedure

## ITS MOST COMMON MEANING:
1. The process of charging tax.

## ITS USE BY LAWYERS:
(-) A detailed assessment of court costs.

The main source of a government's income is taxes levied on its citizens and businesses. Taxation means raising money through taxes and the money so raised.

> *The road improvements will be paid for by taxation of fuel.*

> *Businesses regularly complain that taxation is too high.*

Lawyers use the word *taxation* when there is disagreement between the parties about the costs that should be paid. If agreement cannot be reached, the *receiving party* (the one whose costs will be paid by the *paying party*) draws up a *bill of costs* showing a detailed list of all the costs that were incurred in the litigation (lawyer's fees, court costs, witness fees, out-of-pocket expenses and the like). A court official then assesses the costs item by item, and that process is called **taxation of costs**. The paying party can comment on the claim for costs. The official can be called a Registrar, a **Taxing Master** or a Costs Judge.

## SUMMARY
Citizens pay taxes to the government which raises money through taxation. The amount to be paid is fixed by law as a percentage of income or profit. In law, *taxation* is an

assessment of sums that should properly be paid, and an assessor decides based on their opinion, whether the costs claimed were incurred correctly in a particular case.

# WORD #13: SERVICE

## Type: noun     Category: court procedure

## ITS MOST COMMON MEANING:

1. To be of help or benefit to someone.

## ITS USE BY LAWYERS:

19. The delivery of a formal legal document to a person.

We experience *service* regularly in our daily lives. We enjoy the good service we receive when we visit our favourite restaurant and happily pay the service charge on the bill. We complain about the bad postal service in our area. A bus just went past that said "Sorry, not in service". I have a friend who recently retired after 25 years of public service as a councillor. We may complain about bad service, but overall *service* is a good thing as it is intended to benefit us in some way.

Lawyers use the word *service* to describe the process of delivering an important document to someone, and governments have drawn up a set of rules that govern whether service has been carried out, also called **good service**. Here are some examples.

**Personal service** (or **actual service**) is where a document is served personally on an individual by leaving it with that individual; on a company by leaving it with a person holding a senior position in the company (a director, the treasurer, secretary, chief executive, manager, or other officer); and on a partnership by leaving it with a partner or person who has control or management of the partnership business at its principal place of business.

Rules may also provide for service by post, fax, and email. They may also provide for service out of the jurisdiction, where the defendant, for example, lives in a different country.

Once a document has been served in accordance with the rules, a party may then file a **certificate of service** that sets out how, where and when the person was **served**.

Some contracts state how and where a party may be served, by giving an **address for service** which can be an email address.

Because smartphones are universal, **proof of service** can be by photo or video - the so-called **service by selfie**.

A person who intends to fight proceedings brought by a claimant must file an **acknowledgement of service** and then file a full defence.

## SUMMARY

We know how it feels to receive good service in a restaurant, but may not feel so good when we experience **good service** of a summons to attend court.

# WORD #14: CASE

## Type: noun     Category: court procedure

## ITS MOST COMMON MEANING:
1. A single instance, occurrence, or example of something.

## ITS USE BY LAWYERS:
7a A court action or lawsuit, either civil or criminal, or something that forms sufficient grounds for bringing an action.

7b The evidence offered in court to support a party's claim.

*Case* is one of many words in this collection whose regular meaning differs from its legal meaning when used to describe a court proceeding: see #1 action, #17 cause, #18 matter, #42 proceed.

In general use, a case is a single occurrence or event.

> *We don't usually offer a refund, but we will in this case.*
>
> *In case of fire, break the glass*
>
> *The car crash was not intentional. It was a case of bad judgment.*

To lawyers, a case generally refers to a court action, but it can also be used in specific ways related to court actions. Here are a few of them.

It can describe the overall evidence that one party, such as the prosecutor, has.

> *There was no direct evidence linking the accused with the theft of the car, and the case relied solely on eye witnesses. Thus, the **case against him** was weak.*

At the end of the **prosecution's case** (when all their evidence has been called), the defence can ask the court to rule that there is **no case to answer**, meaning that the prosecution has not **proven their case**. The test at that stage is whether a jury, having heard all of the evidence that has been led by the prosecution, <u>could</u> convict the defendant on that evidence alone. The plea of no case to answer is also used in civil cases if the defendant believes that the claim has no reasonable prospect of success. If the plea succeeds, the judge will stop the case without needing the defence to call its evidence.

Similarly, lawyers refer to a **prima facie case**, that is one that has been supported by sufficient evidence to prove the case if there is no evidence to the contrary. A **prima facie criminal case** is a prosecution case that is strong enough to require the defendant to answer it, and they could be convicted if they don't.

*Case* can be used to refer to a particular court action.

> *The only case on the list this afternoon is Smith v Jones in court 1.*

Or a series of court actions that make up a body of judge-made law, called **case law** (also **caselaw**)

> *The case law on what amounts to dishonesty in theft cases has been growing in the last twenty years.*

Some authorities will bring an action called a **test case**. For example, in civil proceedings, a case can be brought to test a principle of law that, once established, can be applied in other cases. When several claimants have similar claims, one may bring a test case, after which the remainder of the claims may be settled out of court or, if the claim fails, no action will be taken in the other cases.

A **leading case** establishes an important legal principle that other courts are bound to follow.

In both the UK and the US, the courts use a method of hearing called a **case stated**. In the US, it is used in trial cases where a formal written statement of the facts in a case is submitted to the court jointly by the parties so that a decision may be given on the facts without a trial. It is also called a **case agreed on**. In the UK it is a method of appealing on a point of law, whereby a court that made a decision **states a case** for the appeal court to rule on, whether the decision was rightly or wrongly made on the law.

## SUMMARY

In everyday English, a case can be anything: a case of food poisoning, a case of bad luck, a case of poor judgment. In law, *case* is something specific: a matter (#18) being heard (#7) by a court.

## OTHER ENTRIES THAT USE THE WORD CASE

#1 action, #4 stay, #5 find, #7 hear, #8 hold, #10 provide, #17 cause, #18 matter, #31 suit, #43, motion, #45 instance, #46 bench, #49 summary, #59 chambers, #69 bundle, #72 precedent,

# WORD #15: INTEREST

## Type: noun    Category: land and property

## ITS MOST COMMON MEANING:

1. The feeling of wanting to know or learn more about something or someone.

## ITS USE BY LAWYERS:

6. A right, share, or claim to land or property.

Humans have always desired to learn more and discover new things. Individuals are curious and most people have a hobby or an interest in something whether it is photography, art, or cinema. Having an interest in history means spending time reading, researching online and visiting ancient sites and buildings. Interest in something requires the continual spending of time and money to learn about and enjoy the subject.

Lawyers talk about a person with an **interest in land,** which means something different. Once an interest is acquired, the owner does not need to do anything continually to maintain that interest. It is either kept or passed on. I mention in #36 (fee) that I have had a freehold interest in land for many years. I gained it in 2001 and I still have it; I have done nothing to keep it.

An interest in land can take many forms.

A person can have a **life interest** in land, which is an interest in property lasting only during the lifetime of the person to whom it was granted (e.g. where property is given "to John Smith for life").

A person can have a **legal interest** in land, such as a lease for 999 years. A person can have an **equitable interest** in land; for example, a life interest (see above) which is protected by law as land held in trust (#28).

Many interests can be held at the same time (called **concurrent interests**), such as ownership of land by two or more persons, such as a joint tenancy of land by a husband and wife.

A person may have a **beneficial interest**, for example where they do not own the land but they have the advantage of its use. If the land creates income, the beneficial owner, not the actual owner, is taxed as if they own it.

A **future interest** is any right to property that does not take effect immediately. An example is where B has a future interest in property that is held in trust for A for their life and, after they die, for B. This is another example of an **equitable interest** in land.

In a different legal use of the word, a lawyer must always act in **the best interests of their client**. Here *interest* means benefit, advantage or outcome. Sometimes a **conflict of interest** can arise when a lawyer can't act for a client. For example, an employee has been dismissed by a company and they ask a lawyer to sue the company for unfair dismissal. There is a conflict of interest if the law firm also acts for the company.

## SUMMARY

If a person has an interest in something, it is an exercise that is actively carried out over a long period. On the other hand, a legal interest in land is something a person holds by doing nothing until it ends or is transferred to another.

## OTHER ENTRIES THAT USE THE WORD *INTEREST*

#19 term, #27 title, #35 fee, #55 convey, #64 vest

# WORD #16: PRACTICE

Type: noun    Category: lawyers

## ITS MOST COMMON MEANING:
1. Repetition of an activity to gain a skill.

## ITS USE BY LAWYERS:
4. Acting as a qualified lawyer.

In everyday language, the word *practice* refers to the act of repeatedly performing an activity or exercise to improve one's skill in it. For instance, when someone says they *practice* the piano, they play it regularly to get better at it. Similarly, athletes *practice* their sport to enhance their performance, and students *practice* their study skills to do better in their exams. In this way, *practice* is about repetition to improve.

When lawyers talk about *practice*, they are referring to the profession and work they do in the field of law. For example, **legal practice** encompasses the entire profession of being a lawyer, including advising clients, drafting legal documents, and representing clients in court. A **practising lawyer** is actively engaged in the profession, as opposed to one who is qualified but is not currently working as a lawyer, or someone who once acted as a lawyer but has now retired. *Practice* also describes a law firm. I set up my first **legal practice** in 2006. I specialised in the development of land, and it was known as a **planning law practice**. I worked on my own, so it was a **sole practice** and I was known as a **sole practitioner.**

## SUMMARY

Professional pianists need to practice for many hours every day because that is the only way they can maintain a high skill level and seek to get better. To a lawyer, *practice* is just a way to describe what they do, or to refer to the law firm they belong to.

***Please note*** that this word is spelt differently in its noun and verb forms and when used in US and British English. In British English, the noun has the *-ice* ending, and the verb has the *-ise* ending.

> *For forty years I have pract**ised** law in a major law practice.*

A US lawyer would write:

> *For forty years I have pract**iced** law in a major law practice.*

## OTHER ENTRIES THAT USE THE WORD *PRACTICE*

#20 bill, #23 bar, #25 admit, #36 fee, #58 undertaking

# WORD #17: CAUSE

## Type: noun    Category: court procedure

## ITS MOST COMMON MEANING:

1. The source of or reason for an event or action; something that produces a change or result.

## HOW LAWYERS USE THE WORD:

6. A case or court action.

*Cause* has a few meanings in everyday English. It can be a goal, aim or desire which is usually for the benefit of someone else.

> *She committed her life to the cause of ending homelessness in her city.*

It can also mean a ground or a reason for something

> *There is no cause for alarm. Everyone is safe.*

> *The soccer team's win was a cause for celebration.*

> *He has no cause to be disappointed over that performance. It was superb.*

And then there's the most common use, causing something to happen or change.

> *They found the cause of the flooding to be a burst water pipe.*

> *Six years of high rainfall was the direct cause of the flooding.*

Lawyers use *cause* similarly, especially in cases arising from someone's fault. Negligent behaviour can be a **cause of action** *(see #1), for example,* falling asleep while driving and someone is injured as a result. The **cause of action** - the factual basis of the claim - is the set of facts that entitle a person to sue, or a wrongful act that causes harm or loss. The linked word **causation** is also used to describe the link between the action (giving bad financial advice) and the harm (financial loss).

The word *cause* is very different from its everyday use because, to lawyers, it means a court case. It's another way of referring to a set of proceedings in court, or a live case before the courts. A **cause list is** displayed in the public waiting area of a court that lists the cases to be heard that day. The **Daily Cause List** sets out all the cases for trial in the Royal Courts of Justice and its outlying buildings. It also contains the warned list of cases about to be listed for hearing.

> *Your case has appeared in the cause list for next week so we must prepare for the hearing tomorrow.*

Lawyers also use *cause* when applying for costs in a case that has not yet concluded. Suppose there was a preliminary hearing for the production of documents, and the claimant was successful. The court can award **costs in the cause** so that, if there is a later full hearing and the claimant succeeds, the defendant will then pay costs for both the preliminary hearing and the full hearing.

## SUMMARY

*Cause* has several meanings in everyday English: a goal or purpose, a ground or reason, or something that brings about change. Uniquely, lawyers use *cause* as another name for a court case.

See also #1 action

# WORD #18: MATTER

## Type: noun    Category: court procedure

## ITS MOST COMMON MEANING:

1. Something that occupies space, which we can know by using our sense of touch, sight, smell or taste. Something out of which something is made; material.

## ITS USE BY LAWYERS:

12. What a court case is about; a client's instructions for their lawyer to conduct.

The most common meaning of *matter* is something that has mass (weight or substance) and can be experienced using the human senses. Matter can be seen, handled, weighed and measured. It is the opposite of something that exists only in the mind.

Lawyers use the word *matter* entirely differently from its most common meaning and use. To a lawyer, a matter is something that a client asks their lawyer to deal with for them. It could be a will, a divorce, a traffic accident, or the sale of property. The lawyer will open a file and give it a **matter number** on their office system. The lawyer might write to the client after being instructed:

> *Thank you for instructing us to handle your claim for unfair dismissal of employment. This matter will be handled by our employment partner Alex Green whom you met.*

If the case goes to court it could be referred to as a matter, because that is another name for a court case.

> *The only matter on the court list for today is Jones v. Smith, at 10:30 in Court 1.*

Some cases are given the title of "**In the matter of** … " when their subject is a legal issue rather than a claim between two parties. For example, in the case *In the Matter of D (A Child)* [2019] UKSC 42, the United Kingdom Supreme Court decided whether treating a child with challenging behaviour was a breach of his human rights under European Law.

Lawyers can also give it a more restricted meaning when referring to cases before the court.

It can refer to the subject matter of a court action, an issue under consideration, disagreement, or litigation.

> *Your honour, the **matter at issue** in this case is whether the surgeon acted negligently when operating on the claimant.*

One small part of an overall trial could be a **matter of law**, something that a judge alone must decide. In a jury trial, jurors must decide **matters of fact**: was the witness lying when giving evidence? Did the defendant throw the first punch or was he attacked first?

Something might be a **matter of record**: something that has been entered on a court or other public register and can be proven by producing that record.

> *It is a matter of record that Jo Smith died on 2 July 2021 of a heart attack.*

The law also distinguishes between **matters of substance** and **matters of form**. The prosecution must prove that the car was stolen according to the definition of theft. If it was merely borrowed, it was not stolen. That is a matter of substance, so the prosecution must prove that element. Who the car belonged to at the time is irrelevant (a matter of form) even though the property must belong to someone for it to be stolen.

## SUMMARY

In daily English, *matter* is something that can be touched, smelled, tasted and measured. To a lawyer, a *matter* is a case they are asked to advise or work on, or a case before the court.

## OTHER ENTRIES THAT USE THE WORD *MATTER*

#14 case, #59 chambers

# WORD #19: TERM

## Type: noun    Category: general law

## ITS MOST COMMON MEANING:

1. A word or phrase used to describe a thing or to express an idea usually in a specialised area of knowledge.

## ITS USE BY LAWYERS:

7. An estate or interest in land that runs for a set period. Also, a condition of an agreement or contract.

> *The musical term 'sonata' dates back to the sixteenth century.*

A lawyer uses the word *term* in several ways that are different from how it is used in general speech.

*Term* describes a period of time. A 99-year lease is an example of a **term of years** (sometimes called a **term for years**), meaning an interest in land that runs for a fixed period as specified in the lease agreement. A contract of employment that starts on 1 January 2021 and runs for five years is called a **fixed-term contract**.

*Terms* can mean an initial broad agreement, with the details to be added and agreed upon later. In a formal setting, such as negotiating a detailed commercial agreement, the parties might call this first stage drawing up **heads of terms**, where *heads* means *headings,* bullet points or a summary.

*Terms* can also mean the complete agreement:

> *Before I act for you, I must ask you to read and sign my business terms.*

A formal contract is composed of individual terms, for example:

- A *condition* is a term that, if breached, gives the aggrieved party the right either to end the contract or affirm it. In addition, the aggrieved party can also claim damages.

- A *warranty* is a term that, if breached, does not give the aggrieved party the right to terminate the contract; it gives rise only to a right to claim damages.

- An *innominate term* is a category of term that is assessed by reference to the time the breach happens and the significance of the breach at that time.

Terms can be **express terms** (written in the contract itself) or **implied terms** (written into the contract by law, agreement or custom).

Lawyers also use phrases that are called **terms of art**. It means that they do not require any further explanation or definition because there is no disagreement between lawyers about what they mean, but the terms may not be understood or used in the same way by the general public. Here are some that you may come across:

*Hearsay*: Spoken or written evidence made by someone who is not called to give evidence, which the court is asked to accept as evidence for the truth of what is stated.

*Res ipsa loquitur*: [Latin: the thing speaks for itself] A principle applied in the tort of negligence. If an accident has occurred of a kind that usually only happens if someone has been negligent, it may be presumed in the absence of evidence the defendant's negligence caused the accident. For example, a surgeon sewed up a patient but left some scissors inside the body.

*Abatement*: The termination, removal, or destruction of a nuisance.

*Burden of proof*: The duty of a party to litigation to prove a fact in issue. Generally, the burden of proof falls upon the party who asserts the truth of a particular fact (the prosecution or the claimant).

## OTHER ENTRIES THAT USE THE WORD *TERM*
#36 fee, #48 assignment

# WORD #20: BILL

Type: noun    Category: general law

## ITS MOST COMMON MEANING:

1. A written account of money owed for goods or services.

## ITS USE BY LAWYERS:

6. A draft statute before it becomes law. 10. A statement of serious criminal charges.

I have a box file in which I keep my bills: bills for repairs to my car, bills from the electricity company, bills for hotel visits, and bills for meals out. The taxman might need to see if my business expenses have been properly claimed. Then I have the bills (invoices) I have issued to my clients for all those **billable hours** I have spent on client work. The taxman also needs to check my stated income for the year.

I have other bills in my office, too. All lawyers must keep up with changes to the law in their areas of practice. I have recently read the Artificial Intelligence (Regulation) Bill to "make provision for the regulation of Artificial Intelligence; and for connected purposes". It is a **Private Members' Bill** (a Member of Parliament who is not in the Cabinet) and it defines AI to include "generative AI, meaning deep or large language models able to generate text and other content based on the data on which they were trained". The Bill will be debated in the House of Commons and once it has passed through each of its stages it will receive Royal Assent as the Artificial Intelligence (Regulation) Act.

I have another bill in my office: a draft **bill of indictment**. If a case is to be heard by the crown court before a jury, the prosecution must send a draft of the charges that the defendant will face. When the court officer has signed the draft bill, it becomes the indictment on which the defendant is tried.

Lawyers use the word *bill* to apply to many types of formal documents such as:

A **bill of rights:** a document that sets out the fundamental or most important rights of the citizens or residents of a country. For example, the English Bill of Rights of 1689 set out several rights, including freedom of speech for Parliament and prohibiting cruel and unusual punishments. A bill of rights is often part of the constitution of the state and gives courts (sometimes only the supreme court) the power to enforce compliance with such rights. In the USA the Supreme Court can even strike down legislation if it does not comply with the US Bill of Rights.

A **bill of exchange** is similar to a cheque. It is an order in writing addressed by one person (the drawer) to another (the drawee) and signed by the person giving it. The bill of exchange requires the drawee to pay a specified sum of money on demand.

A **bill of lading**: a document acknowledging the receipt of goods for carriage by sea.

## SUMMARY

Bills are important documents to everyone because there are consequences if they are not paid. Lawyers use the word *bill* to refer to other, different kinds of important documents.

## OTHER ENTRIES THAT USE THE WORD *BILL*
#12 taxation, #33 prefer

# WORD #21: NATURAL

## Type: adjective    Category: general law

## ITS MOST COMMON MEANING:
1. According to nature, including human nature.

## ITS USE BY LAWYERS:
Various meanings.


In everyday language, the word *natural* typically refers to things that are found in nature or are not altered by human activity. People use *natural* to describe anything from landscapes and ecosystems to foods and products that are free from artificial ingredients or chemicals. For example, when someone talks about *natural beauty*, they are often referring to unspoiled scenery or a person's appearance without makeup. It is only *natural* to want to feel loved and to feel happy.

Lawyers use the word *natural* in many ways that do not relate to the laws of nature.

1.  A **natural person**. In general use, a natural person does not pretend to be anything other than what they are. In law, a natural person is a human being, in contrast to a limited company, which is a different type of legal person (see #9 person).

2.  A **natural child**. This phrase means a child of parents who are not married to each other.

3.  A **natural citizen**. I was born in England, so I am a natural citizen of the United Kingdom. If I was born in

America and I wanted to be a citizen of the UK, I would have to apply for **naturalisation**, the legal process by which a person acquires a new nationality

4. **Natural rights** automatically belong to a landowner, and violating these rights is an actionable nuisance. The most obvious and important of these is the landowner's right to enjoy their land in its original condition, and not be worsened by the activities of his neighbour, for example by excavation or quarrying operations.

5. **Natural justice**. This phrase is used to refer to rules of fair play that are not natural (in the sense that they are not found in the natural world) but have been developed by humans over the centuries, first in the courts of equity to control the decisions of judges, and then extended to control the decisions of bodies that control a person's status, rights and liabilities. The rules of natural justice include:

   1. All parties have a right to be heard by the person making the decision, and

   2. The decision-maker must be impartial and neutral and must not have a personal interest in the decision's outcome.

## SUMMARY

People use the word *natural* to speak of something that is found in nature and is unspoiled by human interference or change. Lawyers apply the word *natural* in ways that relate to rules that have been created by humans to protect citizenship, property and human rights.

# WORD #22: DETERMINE

## Type: verb    Category: general law

## ITS MOST COMMON MEANING:

1. To settle or decide an argument or question once and for all.

## ITS USE BY LAWYERS:

8. To bring something to an end.

You could say that lawyers commonly use *determine* in both of these senses. Courts *determine* disputes all the time. The purpose of a jury trial is to *determine* a person's guilt or innocence. A coroner's court *determines* someone's cause of death.

Lawyers also use the word *determine* in the sense of bringing something to an end, such as a lease or a contract. Here are some examples under English law of how a landlord may determine a lease:

1.  Breach of an agreement by the tenant to repair the property,

2.  Persistent failure by the tenant to pay rent, or

3.  If the landlord intends to occupy the property.

If the parties agree, a contract may also set out the circumstances in which one party may determine the contract. Here is a sample contract clause that allows for **determination**.

> **DETERMINATION OF THE CONTRACT**. *The Company has the right forthwith to determine this Contract between the Buyer and the Company by written **notice of determination** to the Buyer in any of the following events and for any reason:*
>
> 1. *The Buyer's failure to comply promptly with any of its obligations under this Contract,*
>
> 2. *The Buyer goes into administration or fails to reach an accommodation with any of its creditors,*
>
> 3. *The Buyer's business merges with or is taken over by any other business or undertaking ...*

You will notice the similarity of the words *determination* and *termination*. Both mean the same thing: to bring something to an end.

## SUMMARY

*Determine* is a verb that commonly means to *come to a decision* once and for all. To lawyers *determine* means to *come to an end* once and for all.

## OTHER ENTRIES THAT USE THE WORD *DETERMINE*

#24 discovery, 72 precedent

# WORD #23: BAR

## Type: noun    Category: court procedure

### ITS MOST COMMON MEANING:

1. A long rigid piece of wood, metal, or similar material, typically used as an obstruction, fastening, or weapon.

### ITS USE BY LAWYERS:

9. In the UK, the group name for barristers. In the US, the group name for all lawyers who are qualified to practice in court.

The word *bar* is widely used in English, and its shape explains why it is used this way. Its rectangular shape gives us bar of soap, bar of gold, and bar of chocolate. Then there's the signal strength of our mobile phone.

> *I only have one bar, so I can't make any calls.*

A music score is divided into bars by a thin vertical bar line. A soccer goal has a crossbar. We scan barcodes when we buy groceries.

A bar can act as a barrier, one that prevents access or entry to part of a building, and that is the origin of the use of *bar* to refer to the legal profession. The bar was literally the wooden bar in old courtrooms that separated the public area at the rear from the space near the judges reserved for those having business with the court. A **call to the bar** was just that - a call to occupy and use that space as a lawyer. Like many other common law terms, the phrase originated in England in the Middle Ages, and the call to the bar refers to the summons issued to one who was found to be fit to speak at the bar of the royal courts through experience and qualification.

In the US attorneys are **admitted to the bar** (see #25), whilst in England and Wales barristers are **called to the bar** (#6). From this, the word *bar* was extended to mean the legal profession as a whole, but please note that in England and Wales, **the bar** applies only to barristers. An attorney or a barrister whose ability to practice law is removed is said to have been **disbarred**. As a solicitor, I was not called to the bar but was entered on the roll - a list of people who are allowed to practice as a solicitor in England and Wales. Solicitors are not disbarred, but they are struck off - that is, their name is taken off (or struck off) the list.

## SUMMARY
Lawyers use the word *bar,* a solid object, as a symbol of those recognised to practice law: the bar.

## OTHER ENTRIES THAT USE THE WORD *BAR*
#6 call, #25 admit, #26 audience, #53 counsel, #63 inns

# WORD #24: DISCOVERY

## Type: noun    Category: court procedure

## ITS MOST COMMON MEANING:

1. Something that has been discovered.

## ITS USE BY LAWYERS:

3. Disclosing material to the opposing party in the pre-trial phase of litigation. Also, the material so disclosed.

We use the word *discovery* in general speech to refer to something that has been found out that was not known before, such as the discovery of a new planet, or the discovery of a new cure. Discoveries can be accidental or unplanned.

> *Scientists are excited about the recent discoveries in cancer treatment and control.*

Or it can refer to something that has been looked for and found.

> *Police who have been looking for the missing person have discovered a body on Brighton Beach.*

To US lawyers *discovery* is a process of rounding up what evidence a lawyer already knows they have and producing it to the other party in the proceedings. The act of discovery, in the sense of finding something out, happens as a result of discovery, after receiving and reviewing the other side's discovery documents. Discovery in its general meaning only happens after discovery in its legal sense has happened.

According to the American Bar Association:

*To begin preparing for trial, both sides engage in discovery. This is the formal process of exchanging information between the parties about the witnesses and evidence they will present at trial.*

*Discovery enables the parties to know before the trial begins what evidence may be presented. It's designed to prevent "trial by ambush," where one side doesn't learn of the other side's evidence or witnesses until the trial, when there's no time to obtain answering evidence.*

*One of the most common methods of discovery is to take depositions. A deposition is an out-of-court statement given under oath by any person involved in the case. It is to be used at trial or in preparation for trial. It may be in the form of a written transcript, a videotape, or both.*

*...*

*Other methods of discovery include*

- *A subpoena requiring the other side to produce books, records or other documents for inspection (a subpoena is a written order issued by a court compelling a person to testify or produce certain physical evidence such as records);*

- *having the other side submit to a physical examination; or*

- asking that a document be submitted for examination to determine if it is genuine.

Under UK law, the word *discovery* is no longer used. This process is now called *disclosure*, or *disclosure and inspection of documents,* and the procedure is governed by the Civil Procedure Rules. In criminal cases, the prosecution must provide the initial details of the prosecution case (also called advance information) at the earliest stage and then full disclosure of its case before the jury trial starts.

## SUMMARY

Discovery in its general meaning (one party finding out things they did not know before) only happens after discovery in its legal sense (one party has handed over the discovery documents to the other side).

# WORD #25: ADMIT
## Type: verb    Category: court procedure

### ITS MOST COMMON MEANING:
1. To allow to enter.

### ITS USE BY LAWYERS:
4. To qualify as a lawyer.

The words **admit** and **admission** are used in general English in connection with entering a building for some purpose.

> *Upon admission to the museum, you must go to the second-floor exhibition room.*
>
> *She was admitted to a very good university for science studies.*
>
> *After the accident, the driver was admitted to the hospital for emergency treatment.*

In its legal sense, **admit** and **admission** are used in four main ways:

1. Qualification to practice law,

2. Admitting to a claim or a criminal charge,

3. The introduction of evidence into court, and

4. Giving something formal recognition or proof

## QUALIFICATION TO PRACTICE LAW

In many countries of the world, when a person qualifies to practice law we speak of them as having been **granted admission to practice**, or of **gaining admission to practice law**, or of being **admitted to the profession**, or, commonly **admitted to the bar** (see #23).

Admission is also used to describe a lawyer's length of practice, and hence their qualification and experience. *She has **ten years' admission** at the criminal bar* means she has been a practising criminal lawyer for ten years (also see #6).

## ADMITTING TO WRONGDOING

In a civil case, an admission is a statement by a party that is adverse (harmful) to their case. It may be formal (for example, in a filed statement or document) or informal (said in court). In a criminal case, a guilty plea is **a formal admission** to committing the offence as charged. A defendant may make a statement admitting a set of facts while not admitting guilt.

## ALLOWING EVIDENCE TO BE CONSIDERED BY THE COURT

For evidence to be put before a jury or a judge, it must be relevant to the case being tried and **admissible**. *Admissible* is the adjective form of the verb to admit. Each jurisdiction has rules of evidence that either allow evidence to be admitted, or prevent evidence from being admitted. These are rules of **admissibility** and **inadmissibility** of evidence.

We speak of documents being **admitted into evidence**, and documents being **admitted as evidence** of the defendant's guilt.

## FORMAL RECOGNITION OR PROOF

When a person dies having made a will, the process of validating the will and appointing executors to carry out the testator's wishes is called probate. A will is **admitted to probate** for this purpose.

If a defendant's criminal case is adjourned and they are given bail to appear at court at a later date, they are **admitted to bail** to appear on that day.

In the USA there are **admitted companies**. These are insurance companies that are registered in one state but are admitted by another state to offer insurance contracts there. These companies provide **admitted insurance**.

## SUMMARY

A person is given the right to enter a building if they are admitted to it. Lawyers are not given the right to enter a building; instead, they are admitted into their profession. An admitted lawyer is someone who is allowed to practice law.

# WORD #26: AUDIENCE

Type: noun    Category: court procedure

## ITS MOST COMMON MEANING:

1. A group of people attending a play or film.

## ITS USE BY LAWYERS:

(-) A lawyer's ability to appear before a court.

Last night, I was in the audience at my local cinema to see a live broadcast of *Macbeth*. I could see the theatre audience on the screen and I was part of the audience at the cinema.

Lawyers use the word *audience* to refer to their ability or right to appear in court. Not all countries use the phrase **rights of audience**, but the UK does. Here, the legal profession is divided into two main branches and not all lawyers can appear before all courts. Barristers are expert advocates and they have an automatic right of audience before all courts. Solicitors can appear in the lowest-level criminal and civil courts. Other very limited rights of audience are available automatically, and others have to be earned.

There is even a statutory definition of a *right of audience*.

Paragraph 3(1) of Schedule 2 to the Legal Services Act 2007 says:

> A "right of audience" means the right to appear before and address a court, including the right to call and examine witnesses.

In the US, there is no phrase equivalent to **right of audience**, because there is no distinction between types of lawyers such as solicitors and barristers in the UK. US attorneys may appear in the state courts for the state in which they were admitted, but the right to appear before federal courts, such as the United States district courts or United States courts of appeal is not automatic. In general, an attorney is admitted to the bar (see #23) of these federal courts upon payment of a fee and taking an oath of admission. An attorney must apply to each district separately. An attorney wishing to practice before the Supreme Court of the United States must apply to do so must be admitted to the bar of the highest court of a state for three years, must be sponsored by two attorneys already admitted to the Supreme Court bar, must pay a fee and must take either a spoken or written oath.

In all jurisdictions, a live court case is called a "hearing" (see #7), and the defendant has a right to be "heard". There is a word link between "hearing" and "audience". We use the word *audio* to refer to recorded sound such as a digital file, a CD or vinyl record, and *audio* is a Latin word meaning *I hear. Audiens* means *hearing* in Latin, that is the thing our ears do. The meaning of *theatre audience* (the people who are hearing the performance) and *right of audience* (being heard by the judge) are not so far apart after all.

## SUMMARY
An audience in the theatre sees and hears the performance on stage. But a lawyer has the right of audience (to be seen and heard) in court.

# WORD #27: TITLE

## Type: noun    Category: land and property

## ITS MOST COMMON MEANING:
1. The name of a book, play, film etc.

## ITS USE BY LAWYERS:
9. A right of ownership of land.

The primary meaning of *title* is the name of something, such as a novel, a play or a poem. It's a convenient way to refer to a work that marks it as unique or different from everything else. The title of my favourite film is *Shakespeare in Love*. You would know immediately which film I mean because there is no other film with that title on Amazon or the IMDb website.

To a lawyer, *title* means a couple of things:

1. *Title* describes a person's legal ownership of property, usually land, and

2. *Title* is how a person proves their ownership of the property.

I own the house in which I live, and my **title to** the land is an **absolute title,** meaning I have exclusive ownership. I **hold the title** in fee simple absolute (see #36). I can prove my ownership by showing you the relevant **title document**, which in this case is a copy of the Land Registry entry for the property which states:

Title Number: DM396911

A: Property Register

This register describes the land and estate **comprised in the title**.

DEVON: EXETER

1   The Freehold land shown edged with red on the plan of the above **title** filed at the Registry and being 15 Old Bakery Close, Exwick, Exeter (EX4 2UZ).

B: Proprietorship Register

This register specifies the **class of title** and identifies the owner. It contains any entries that affect the right of disposal.

Title absolute

1     PROPRIETOR: GRAHAM RONALD GOVER of 15 Old Bakery Close, Exwick, Exeter EX4 2UZ.

Historically, **title to land** was proven by a written document such as a deed of transfer, but other people may also have an **interest in the land** (see #15), for example, a tenant under a lease, or where a person has lent money to enable the land to be purchased (an interest by way of mortgage). A person may have **title to land** (meaning ownership, and the ability to transfer it to another) and other people may have different kinds of **interest in** the land.

In both the UK and the US, title **to** land and interests **in** land are registered, and a person who may want to purchase the land can search the register to find out who **has title** and who else is interested in it.

## SUMMARY

I *have* a title; it is Mr Graham Gover. But I *own* the title absolute in the land where I live.

## OTHER ENTRIES THAT USE THE WORD *TITLE*
#30 completion, #36 fee, #55, convey, #56 deed

# WORD #28: TRUST

Type: noun     Category: land and property

## ITS MOST COMMON MEANING:

1. Reliance on and confidence in the character, ability, strength, or truth of someone or something.

## ITS USE BY LAWYERS:

7. An arrangement in which a person (a trustee) holds property as its nominal owner for the good of one or more people (beneficiaries).

Because trust law is so broad and varies from country to country, no attempt has been made to cover the subject in this book or to introduce the vocabulary or word associations here. I have included the word as one of the 75 and given it the briefest of introductions.

A trust is the right to the beneficial enjoyment of property to which another person holds the legal title. It is a property interest held by one person (the trustee) at the request of another (the settlor) for the benefit of a third party (the beneficiary). For a trust to be valid, it must involve specific property, reflect the settlor's intentions, and be created for a lawful purpose. The two primary types of trusts are **private trusts** and **charitable trusts**. There should always be a **declaration of trus**t that sets out the purpose of the trust, as well as a **trust deed** or other **trust instrument** (#37) if land is included in the settlement.

## SUMMARY

Trust is the confidence that I have placed in someone else. Land is placed in a trust for someone else's benefit.

## OTHER ENTRIES THAT USE THE WORD *TRUST*
#15 interest, #37, instrument, #56 deed

# WORD #29: DELIVERY

Type: noun     Category: land and property

## ITS MOST COMMON MEANING:

1. The act of physically moving items (goods, parcels, mail) from one place to another.

## ITS USE BY LAWYERS:

7. The act of giving control or possession of property from one person to another.


Pizza Hut Tweeted on 9 September 2013 that the first ever online purchase was of a Pizza Hut pizza in 1994. From that humble start, the business of online ordering and delivery of food has mushroomed (sorry!) to a global industry valued at $294 billion in 2021 and has been called a food-delivery revolution. Using websites or mobile phone apps, a customer can order and pay for food directly from a restaurant, and delivered to them by a courier driving a car or riding a motorbike or pedal cycle.

In the legal world, delivery can take place even where nothing moves at all. For example, suppose that a warehouse contains 1000 sacks of rice. The owner agrees to sell them to a buyer for $10,000. Upon receipt of the money, the seller sends the warehouse keys to the buyer. At that moment, the rice has been **delivered to** the buyer, but it remains in the warehouse, ready for collection by the buyer at some future date. *Delivery* simply means the transfer of control or possession from one person to another.

Documents known as deeds (see #56) also involve the process of *delivery*. The well-known phrase "signed, sealed and delivered" refers to deeds that are legal instruments in writing that pass or create interests in land. The parties sign them; they are sometimes sealed and always **delivered** by one party to the other. As in the example above, copies of the document are seldom moved around for the deeds to take effect. Copies are shared after execution (#50) and completion (#30) so that each party has a copy for their records, but the deeds are in effect **delivered** once they have been executed by all the parties. Distribution of the deeds takes place well after the deeds have been **delivered**.

## SUMMARY

In the real world, delivery means moving property from one *place* to another. In the legal world, delivery means transferring property from one *person* to another. Property can remain in the same place and still be delivered.

## OTHER ENTRIES THAT USE THE WORD *DELIVERY*

#13 service, #56 deed

# WORD #30: COMPLETION
Type: noun     Category: land and property

## ITS MOST COMMON MEANING:
1. The process of finishing anything that has been started.

## ITS USE BY LAWYERS:
10. The moment when the sale and purchase of a property takes place.

Some things have a beginning and an end. The building of the Great Wall of China began in about 400 B.C and was completed in about A.D. 1600, taking 2,000 years.

Mini Sky City in Hunan Province has 57 floors and was completed in 19 days, in 2015. That's three floors a day.

The first Nightingale Hospital in England, built in 2020 in response to the COVID-19 pandemic and providing 4,000 beds, was completed in just nine days.

For lawyers, completion takes place in an instant. Lawyers in the UK* refer to **completion taking place** on a given day, even though the process for the sale and purchase of land begins before and concludes well after **completion day** itself. Take, for example, the purchase of a house. Sometime before completion, the buyer and seller exchange contracts for the sale and purchase of the house. There is a point at which the signed contracts of sale are exchanged by the seller and buyer's respective conveyancing lawyers (see #55). Once the contracts have been exchanged, the seller and the buyer are both legally obliged to see the transaction through to completion.

On **completion day**, the purchase money is transferred to the seller's lawyer, and when this has happened, the sale and purchase take place. At this point, the property legally belongs to the buyer. The sale is completed at that moment. The seller must then leave the property and the buyer may move in.

Although completion has occurred, the conveyancing process continues. The seller's lawyer draws up the title deed and the completed transfer deed and sends them to the buyer's solicitor. If the seller has a mortgage on the property, it must be discharged from the sale money. The buyer has to pay Stamp Duty Land Tax to the government. The Land Registry records are updated with details of the new owner and any mortgage company's details.

*Completion* happened on **completion day** when the title was transferred from seller to buyer, but the conveyancing process continues for many days after that day.

*In the US, the process of *completion* is called *closure*, so this is another example of an everyday word being used differently. *Closure* means the act of stopping operations or shutting down a business, but for US lawyers it means the same as completion.

## SUMMARY
In life, when something is finished, the job is complete. Lawyers use the word *completion* to mean that the sale of land has taken place and title has been transferred to the buyer. The conveyancing process continues well after completion.

## OTHER ENTRIES THAT USE THE WORD *COMPLETION*
#29 delivery, #55 convey

# WORD #31: SUIT
### Type: noun    Category: court procedure

## ITS MOST COMMON MEANING:
1. Clothes made up of matching items.

## ITS USE BY LAWYERS:
5 A civil proceeding; lawsuit.  6 The act or process of suing in a court of law.

In everyday language, the word *suit* refers to a set of clothes. Most people think of a suit as a matching jacket and trousers (or skirt), often worn with a shirt and tie, which is typically worn for occasions like business meetings, weddings, or other formal events. Suits are seen as a symbol of professionalism and style in many cultures, and they come in various styles, colours, and fabrics to suit different tastes and occasions.

However, lawyers use the word *suit* in a very different way. In the legal world, *a suit* (also known as a lawsuit) is a case brought by someone who feels wronged by another. When a person **files suit** (not *files a suit*), they are asking the court to resolve a dispute, often seeking some form of compensation or remedy for the harm they believe they have suffered. For example, if someone is injured in a car accident and believes the other driver is at fault, they might **file suit** to get money for medical bills and other damages.

The word *sue* is the verb form of *suit:* a person sues another, and the court action is called a suit. The person bringing the case is a **suitor**, and the case can be a **suit in contract**, a **blackmail suit,** or a **civil suit**.

## SUMMARY

A lawyer may wear a suit to go to court, but to a lawyer, a suit is a court action.

## OTHER ENTRIES THAT USE THE WORD *SUIT*

#40 complaint

# WORD #32: CONSTRUCTION

## Type: noun    Category: general law

### ITS MOST COMMON MEANING:

1. Something that has been built, such as a building, a road or a bridge.

### ITS USE BY LAWYERS:

4. The meaning or interpretation of a legal text.


If someone told you that they work in construction, you would imagine they are part of a team that builds tall buildings, assembles steel girders, lays bricks, and uses their hands and power tools to create large structures.

When lawyers talk about construction, they describe a process that goes on in their minds. What is the meaning of this statute, this case, or this document, and how can I explain it to my client or propose its meaning to the court?

All law, whether it is a statute, a contract or a court decision, is open to interpretation. Different people will understand the meaning of words in different ways. This is also the case when the language used in the document is unclear or ambiguous, or when the intent of the writer is not plain. A lawyer is always in search of the construction of a case, a section in a statute or a phrase in a contract.

For example, when a court interprets a statute, it may use a narrow construction, which means it sticks closely to the literal meaning of the words used. Or they may use a **broad construction**, which means they interpret the law more widely, in a way that is consistent with what they believe the author intended.

For instance, in the case of *Muscarello v. United States* (1998), the Supreme Court was asked to interpret the phrase "carries a firearm". The court could have used a narrow construction, which would have meant that the phrase only applied to people who physically carried a firearm in their hands. Instead, they used a broad construction, which meant that the phrase could also apply to people who had a firearm in the locked glove compartment or the boot (trunk) of their car that was nearby.

Courts have developed various **canons of construction** (or **rules of construction**), which vary from country to country.

Another difference between the word *construction* and how it is used differently by lawyers is in its verb form. A builder *constructs* a house; a lawyer *construes* a statute.

## SUMMARY

Construction is carried out by builders using their hands, resulting in a physical building. Construction is carried out by lawyers in their minds, and the result is an interpretation, an idea, of what the author intended by the words they used.

# WORD #33: PREFER

## Type: verb    Category: criminal law

## ITS MOST COMMON MEANING:

1. To like one thing more than another

## ITS USE BY LAWYERS:

3. To bring a criminal charge against an accused.

I prefer running to cycling as a way of keeping fit. My wife prefers cycling. We are all different. No one would prefer being taken to court for a criminal offence, but somehow the word *prefer* is used to describe the process of charging a person with a crime.

The glossary of the English Criminal Procedure Rules 2020 defines *prefer* as "to bring or lay a charge or indictment". The formal charge starts as a draft bill of indictment (see #20) and becomes the indictment when it is **preferred before** the Crown Court and the defendant pleads guilty or not guilty.

Charges are said to be **preferred against** the defendant, and the charges are called the **preferment**.

*Prefer charges* is not to be confused with *proffer charges* or a *proffer agreement* (a US term), where the individual is under investigation or has been charged with a crime, and wants to offer information to law enforcement authorities in exchange for some benefit, such as dropped or reduced charges or an agreement for a lower sentence.

## SUMMARY

What would you prefer; having charges preferred against you, or not having charges preferred against you?

# WORD #34: ISSUE

## Type: noun   Category: general law

### ITS MOST COMMON MEANING:

1. Something being discussed or in dispute.

### ITS USE BY LAWYERS:

7. Children.

> *The two biggest issues in the last election were immigration and education*
>
> *My biggest issue with my neighbour is his noisy parties late at night.*

Lawyers also use the word *issue* in the same way, which is not surprising when much of legal work involves disputes leading to litigation.

> *The **point at issue** between us is not whether my client took £5,000 from your client's house. The issue is whether she acted dishonestly or believed it was her own money. That is the only issue the court will have to decide.*

But the chief way that lawyers use the word *issue* differently is to use it to refer to children. In a will you may see these words:

> *To each of my issue who survive me, I leave the sum of £1,000,000 free of tax.*

However, the problem with this word is that it can be ambiguous. A line of cases says *issue* means all descendants, not just children. For that reason, it is safer to use the word *child* or *children*. The word *issue* is also a bit dated and is only used that way by lawyers.

*He died without issue* means he died without children (or other descendants). This is also called a **failure of issue** or **for want of issue**.

## SUMMARY

In daily life, an issue is a problem, a point of discussion or a complaint. To a lawyer, admittedly one who uses very old language, an issue is a child or children.

## OTHER ENTRIES THAT USE THE WORD *ISSUE*

#8 hold, #18 matter, #19 term, #43 motion

# WORD #35: SENTENCE
Type: noun    Category: court procedure

## ITS MOST COMMON MEANING:
1. A group of words, usually consisting of a subject, an object and a verb, that makes sense on its own, to create a statement, ask a question, or give a command.

## ITS USE BY LAWYERS:
2. The decision of the court as to the punishment to be given to a person who is guilty of a criminal offence.

I would say that both meanings are well-known and understood and do not need to be explained here. It is, however, another good example of how the word *sentence* is used so very differently. On the one hand, it is just a collection of spoken or written words. On the other, it can be the order that a person goes to prison for the rest of their life.

## SUMMARY
The sentence of the court can be stated in a single sentence.

*You will pay a fine of £1,000 within seven days.*

# WORD #36: FEE

## Type: noun    Category: land and property

## ITS MOST COMMON MEANING:
1. Payment asked for by a professional for their services.

## ITS USE BY LAWYERS:
3. A legal interest in land.


*Fee* is one of those words that I associate with lawyers in both its meanings. Lawyers charge a fee for their work. It's how they earn their income. A legal practice is divided into those who generate fees (the fee earners) and those who support them in their fee earning. Law firms set their fee income for the coming year. Lawyers agree fees in advance with their clients or agree to a fee structure for more complicated work.

The other way in which lawyers use the word *fee* is to describe a legal interest in a piece of land. The subject of legal interest in land (see #15) is long and complicated, so let me give you an example from real life. In fact, my real life because I own some land - it's the land my house sits on. If I needed to prove my interest in that land (for instance, if you were interested in buying it) I would show you a copy of the entry in the Land Registry for that land. It shows the Registered Owner to be Graham Ronald Gover (that's me). The land is identified by a red line on the filed plan and is called *freehold land*, which means it is not held by me under a lease for a fixed term of years. In the Proprietorship part, the owner with *title absolute* is me, Graham Ronald Gover.

As the freehold owner of the land with title absolute a lawyer would say that I own the land **in fee simple**, sometimes called **fee simple absolute in possession**.

*Fee simple* indicates ownership that is not liable to end and return to its owner upon my death, or at the end of a fixed period, or if I die without any children. *Absolute* means that my rights are not subject to any condition or not liable to end on the occurrence of any event. *In possession* means that my rights are immediate, they exist now. The land is mine, nobody else has any interest in it, and I can leave it in my will to anybody I choose.

This is the base meaning of *fee*: it is real property (see #3) that I can enjoy in my lifetime and I can leave it in my will. It is the strongest and most secure interest in land.

## SUMMARY
My lawyer charged me a fee for transferring the fee simple in land to me.

## OTHER ENTRIES THAT USE THE WORD *FEE*
#27 title

# WORD #37: INSTRUMENT

## Type: noun    Category: general law

## ITS MOST COMMON MEANING:

1. A device for making music

## ITS USE BY LAWYERS:

7. A legal document that sets out rights, duties and requirements.

In everyday English, the word *instrument* commonly refers to tools or devices used for a specific purpose, often within the context of music or tasks requiring precision or skill. For most people, an instrument conjures images of musical devices like guitars, pianos, or violins, which produce sound and music. Alternatively, it can refer to tools like surgical instruments, which are used by professionals in medical fields for operations, or scientific instruments like microscopes and thermometers, essential for conducting experiments and measurements. In these contexts, *instrument* embodies the notion of a tangible, physical object designed for a particular function or task.

In contrast, lawyers use the term *instrument* more abstractly. In the legal realm, an *instrument* refers to a formal written document that records a legally enforceable act or agreement. The term *instrument* covers contracts, deeds, statutes, wills, warrants, schemes, letters patent, rules, regulations, and bylaws; in fact, any written or printed legal document that may have to be interpreted by the Courts.

Although it has a very wide legal meaning and application, it is also used in specific ways.

In the UK, an Act of Parliament may authorise more detailed laws to be made by a government official after the Act takes effect. This is called **delegated legislation** and can be done by **Statutory Instrument**.

A cheque is a form of **negotiable instrument**: a document that creates an obligation to pay a sum of money.

An official document such as a passport, a postage stamp or a birth certificate that has been altered to commit a crime is termed a **false instrument**.

A **trust instrument** is a deed (#see 56) under which property is vested (#64) in trustees upon trust (#28) to apply it for the benefit of the beneficiaries specified in the deed.

## SUMMARY

The difference in the use of the word *instrument* between laypeople and legal professionals lies in its tangible versus intangible nature. While the general public associates instruments with physical objects used for specific tasks, lawyers view instruments as documents that serve as tools for creating and enforcing legal rights and obligations.

## OTHER ENTRIES THAT USE THE WORD *INSTRUMENT*

#28 trust, #deed

# WORD #38: RELIEF
## Type: noun    Category: court procedure

## ITS MOST COMMON MEANING:

1. The removal of any burden, evil, pressure or stress. The feeling that comes with it.

## ITS USE BY LAWYERS:

15. An order of the court that benefits the claimant; the remedy that was asked for in the claim.

> *At last, my exams are over. What a relief!*
>
> *Jamie was found alive and well, which was a great relief to his parents.*
>
> *The tablets acted quickly to give instant pain relief.*

Relief is a strong emotion when pain, stress, or hardship is over. The greater the stress, the greater the emotion of feeling relieved.

To lawyers, *relief* is not an emotion, it is a remedy that is requested of the court for the benefit of the claimant. In civil proceedings the **relief sought** is the whole purpose of bringing the proceedings, so anything that the court orders is *relief*. It can be one or more of the following:

A *declaration*: a ruling by the judge on the lawfulness of something such as a will, a decision by a court or tribunal, or someone's rights.

*Mandatory order*: a direction by the court to a lower court to carry out its lawful duty.

*Injunction*: also known as **injunctive relief**, an order of the court that requires a person to do, or not do, something that is specified in the order.

*Damages*: financial compensation for loss suffered as a result of the defendant's behaviour.

There are many more available **reliefs**. And that is an example of the further difference between the general and the legal use of the word. It is commonly used in the plural form *reliefs* when used by lawyers, but not in its general use (you get a feeling of relief).

One of the papers served in a civil claim is the **prayer for relief**, in which the claimant requests the relief that is sought. It is also referred to as the **relief gateway**.

## SUMMARY

It must be quite a relief to get the relief you requested in the claim: $1,000,000 in damages after five years in court.

# WORD #39: PRESENTS

Type: noun    Category: contracts

## ITS MOST COMMON MEANING:

1. Gifts usually given to celebrate a birthday or Christmas.

## ITS USE BY LAWYERS:

(-) The document before you, the one you are reading.

Lawyers have a bad habit of using precedents (see #72). Well, not so much using them as the habit of following the precedent's wording without thinking, or worrying about the risk of departing from a text that has been used for many years.

I very recently received a draft deed from a lawyer employed by a local authority in London that included this clause:

> *IN WITNESS whereof with the intent that **these presents** should be executed as a Deed the parties hereto have duly executed the same the day and year first before written.*

What does "these presents" mean? Is the deed a gift from the local authority? Sadly no. It simply means "this document", the one you are reading.

I do not doubt that the lawyer was just filling in the blanks on a precedent form to make the document apply to the particular case the deed was written for, without thinking about the centuries-old words and phrases elsewhere in the document.

Lawyers have used the words "these presents" since the 14th century, and are still often found in the very sexist phrase:

| *know all men by these presents ...*

"These presents" can easily be replaced by "this document" with no loss of meaning or understanding.

## SUMMARY

The best present you can give a lawyer is the gift of persuading him not to use the word "presents" in a legal document.

# WORD #40: COMPLAINT

Type: noun    Category: court procedure

## ITS MOST COMMON MEANING:

1. The act of complaining about something.

## ITS USE BY LAWYERS:

4. The document that commences civil proceedings in the US courts, and the magistrates' courts in England and Wales.

When was the last time you complained about something? Maybe it was about poor service at the dry cleaners, or food at the restaurant that was cold when it should have been hot, or your taxi was 20 minutes late. Then you know about making a complaint.

This phrase has a wholly different meaning to a lawyer because a complaint is not a negative comment about food, but how some civil proceedings are started. In the US this is called **filing a complaint**, and in England and Wales it is called **making a complaint**.

In the US the procedure is governed by the Federal Rules of Civil Procedure. It specifies that a civil lawsuit begins when the plaintiff (the party bringing the suit) files a complaint with the appropriate federal district court. The complaint is a legal document that outlines the basis of the court's jurisdiction, the allegations against the defendant, and the specific relief or damages the plaintiff seeks. Once the complaint is filed, the court issues a summons to be served on the defendant, notifying them of the lawsuit and outlining the steps they must take to respond. This process ensures that the defendant is given fair notice and an opportunity to defend the allegations.

In England, most civil cases are dealt with by the civil courts and cases are started by filing a claim. A magistrates' court largely deals with criminal cases, but it also has a limited civil caseload and proceedings are started by making a complaint. As in the US, the complaint must specify its legal basis, and a summons is then issued for the defendant to appear before the magistrates' court.

## SUMMARY

A complaint can be spoken or in writing and is an adverse comment or criticism. To a lawyer, a complaint is always in writing, and it is how some civil proceedings are started.

# WORD #41: WHEREAS
Type: conjunction    Category: contracts

## ITS MOST COMMON MEANING:
1. In contrast; although; to the contrary; on the other hand.

## ITS USE BY LAWYERS:
(-) It is true that.

*Whereas* is one of those words that lawyers use in the opposite way to everyone else. It is used in general speech to compare or contrast two different things.

> *Doctors' pay rose by 10% last year whereas nurses' pay went down by 2% in real terms.*
>
> *John loves holidays abroad, whereas his wife prefers to stay at home.*

However, lawyers use the word *whereas* to link things that are true, rather than to contrast things that are different, and to say that because these things are so, this document has in consequence been drawn up.

In a contract, for example, there may be a section that sets out some facts that are the background to or the setting of the agreement and the reasons for it being made. This may also be called the *recitals* (see #75) or *background.*

Take for example the first section of a service contract between a software company and a programmer that reads like this:

*Agreement between:*

*SoftgenX plc (The Company) and*

*William Victor Fence (the Programmer)*

*Whereas*

*1. The Company is considering a national expansion of its AI capability, more fully described in the Business Plan.*

*2. The Programmer is experienced in providing coding services in an AI environment.*

*3. The Company wishes to commission the Programer to investigate the potential market for the products described in the Business Plan and prepare a report and recommendations, as described in the Specifications. The Programmer is willing to provide such services, all by the terms of this Agreement.*

In this case, the word *whereas* is not used to show that the parties disagree with each other. On the contrary, all points 1 - 3 are agreed and are the reasons why the parties want to and need to enter into the agreement.

## SUMMARY

In daily speech, *whereas* is used to link together two things that contrast with each other because they are different or contradictory. Lawyers use *whereas* to link ideas and statements that are true, accurate and consistent.

# WORD #42: PROCEED

## Type: verb　　Category: court procedure

### ITS MOST COMMON MEANING:
1. To move forward.

### ITS USE BY LAWYERS:
3. To start or continue a legal action.

In its simplest sense to *proceed* means to move or travel forward.

> *To get to the registration desk, proceed down the corridor then enter the third door on the left*

> *The road surface is uneven: proceed with caution.*

It describes a person's physical movement forward.

If you simply add a preposition, *proceed* now describes the commencement of legal action.

> *We decided to **proceed against** the restaurant because we all had food poisoning after eating the shellfish.*

The same is true of the noun form *proceedings*. In daily use, proceedings can be used to refer to the actions of a public body.

> *The clerk, John Smith, kept records of the Highways Committee's proceedings for 20 years before his retirement.*

But lawyers use it to describe a legal action.

> *For minor criminal offences, proceedings must be commenced within six months.*
>
> *She **started proceedings against** the City Council because the state of the road wrecked her car.*

A person **starts** or **brings proceedings**. These can be **child-protection proceedings**, **civil proceedings** or **criminal proceedings.** They can be proceedings *for* something, such as **proceedings for damages,** or proceedings *in* a particular area of law such as **proceedings in libel** or **in negligence**.

## OTHER ENTRIES THAT USE THE WORD *PROCEEDINGS*

#4 stay, #9 person, #11 information, #13 service, #14 case, #17 cause, #24 discovery, #38 relief, #40 complaint, #43 motion, #45 instance

# WORD #43: MOTION

## Type: noun    Category: court procedure

## ITS MOST COMMON MEANING:

1. The activity or process of continually changing position or moving from one place to another.

## ITS USE BY LAWYERS:

6. A procedure to bring a limited, contested issue before a court for decision: a request to a judge to decide some point in the case.

Do you like going to the movies? I do, and in a typical year, I see about 50 films at the cinema. Some of them are what Hollywood calls a "major motion picture," a film with famous actors that cost millions of dollars.

Do you know why they are called movies or motion pictures? The words move and motion are very similar. With the invention of the moving image (a series of still photographs passing across a beam of light so rapidly that the still images create the effect of movement), new words, such as motion picture and movie, came into use. Images that did not move were called *stills*, and images that moved were called *movies* or *motion* pictures.

In everyday use, the word *motion* refers to movement, something that is always changing position or moving in a particular way.

However, to lawyers, a *motion* is simply an application to the court. In England and Wales, the word *motion* has now been replaced with the word *application* in the rules of the civil court. *Motion* is commonly used in the US courts, and the following text is based on US procedures.

A motion is a procedural device to bring a limited, contested issue (see #34) before a court for a decision. It is a request to the judge to decide the case or part of it. Motions may be made at any point in the proceedings, and federal and local court rules regulate that right. The party requesting the motion is the **moving party** or **movant**. The party opposing the motion is the **nonmoving party** or **nonmovant**.

Examples are:

A **motion to dismiss**: used when a claim has been started after a time bar (statute of limitations) or if there is a defect in bringing the proceedings.

A **motion for summary judgment** asks the court to decide that the evidence supports a ruling in favour of the moving party.

A **motion for a directed verdict** asks the court to rule that the plaintiff or prosecutor has not proven the case and that the defence does not need to present evidence. If granted, the court would dismiss the case.

A **motion to set aside judgment** asks the court to vacate or nullify a judgment or verdict.

See also #44 move.

## SUMMARY

In its everyday sense, *motion* is all about moving from place to place. In legal use, a motion is not about movement at all. It is simply a request to the court.

# WORD #44: MOVE

## Type: verb    Category: court procedure

## ITS MOST COMMON MEANING:
1. To move or take something from one place to another; to change location or position.

## ITS USE BY LAWYERS:
12. To ask the court to do something.

See #43 motion for a detailed explanation of the related words *move* and *motion*.

*Move* is the informal way of referring to an application to the court, and is the verb form of the noun *motion*.

| *Move to strike, your Honour*

is an informal way for an attorney to speak to the judge

| *I am making a motion to strike.*

A **move to strike** is a request by one party in a United States trial requesting that the presiding judge orders the removal of all or part of the opposing party's pleading to the court or the removal from the court's record of evidence of some of the witness evidence so that the jury will ignore it.

To **move the court** is another informal way of referring to a formal request of the court.

| *The Appellant moved the court for a new trial.*

If the court agrees to act in the way requested, you can say

*The **court was moved** to grant a new trial*

For a summary, see #43 motion, and the summary there.

# WORD #45: INSTANCE

## Type: noun     Category: court procedure

## ITS MOST COMMON MEANING:

1. An example of, or a case that, illustrates a point.

## ITS USE BY LAWYERS:

3. A step or stage in legal proceedings.

In everyday language, the word *instance* is often used to refer to a specific example or occurrence of something. When people talk about an *instance*, they usually mean a particular situation, event, or case that illustrates a broader idea or pattern. For example, someone might say,

> *The trains at this station are rarely on time. For instance, yesterday my train was two hours late.*

Here, *instance* simply means an individual example of a late-running train that is part of a larger picture of delays on the rail network.

In contrast, in the legal world, *instance* refers to a particular stage proceedings (see #42) have reached. For example, the term **first instance** describes the initial trial or hearing of a case in a lower court, where the facts are examined, and a verdict or judgment is given. If the case is appealed, it moves to a higher court, and this new phase may be referred to as the **appellate instance**. In this context, *instance* signifies the different levels or stages of judicial proceedings.

Legal proceedings start or are first heard in **a court of first instance**. Once a decision has been made, the case may move to a higher court for an appeal or a legal challenge to the decision. In the US, in the federal court system, a federal district court is the **court of first instance**, whereas the Supreme Court is the **court of last instance**. For criminal cases in England, the **court of first instance** is the magistrates' court, and the **court of last instance** is the Supreme Court. There is no higher court than the Supreme Court in each jurisdiction. There is only a first and a last instance: there is no second or third instance court.

## SUMMARY

In general English, an instance is an example. In legal English, an instance is a stage at which a case is heard as it moves through the appeal system.

# WORD #46: BENCH

Type: noun    Category: court procedure

## ITS MOST COMMON MEANING:
1. A long, usually wooden, seat with or without a back, for two or more people.

## ITS USE BY LAWYERS:
3. A judge or magistrates while presiding at court. 5. Collectively, all magistrates and judges.

We commonly see benches in public places, such as parks, gardens, or beaches, which are used for rest. The use of the word bench to refer to the presiding judge dates back to the fourteenth century when the judge would sit on a raised bench while presiding in court, and the two meanings (the judge and the seat they occupy) have become one. The direction for lawyers to **approach the bench** is for the judge to speak with the lawyers quietly so that no one else can hear. Comments made **by the bench** are those spoken by the sitting judge or magistrates.

The term **bench trial** is used when a judge decides a criminal case without a jury.

A court issues a **bench warrant** if someone fails or refuses to appear as a defendant or witness.

The meaning has been widened to refer to a particular court. The judges of the United States Court of Appeals for the Fifth Circuit are known as the **Fifth Circuit bench**. England has the **King's Bench Division of the High Court,** which reviews the legal decisions of the lower criminal courts.

Even wider, it refers to all judges and magistrates (the judiciary).

| *Jo Smith left the bar and **joined the bench** in 1970.*

Sometimes, **elevated to the bench** is used in this way.

## SUMMARY

Benches are dead pieces of furniture. They don't speak, send people to prison or decide points of law, but somehow, *the bench* can, when used by lawyers.

## OTHER ENTRIES THAT USE THE WORD *BENCH*

#5 find, #54 crown

# WORD #47: NOTICE

## Type: noun    Category: general law

## ITS MOST COMMON MEANING:

1. The act of observing or paying attention to something. Information or a warning given in writing

## ITS USE BY LAWYERS:

(-) A type of knowledge of something specific, something a person did or should have known.

I am writing this on a train travelling through Sweden, and I am taking notice of how busy the train is, how pretty the passing countryside is and how similar the buildings are to those in my home town. There are many notices in the carriage about safety and train facilities, and because this is Sweden, all the notices are also in English. I have duly taken notice of what to do in an emergency, and where the bistro carriage is.

In law, it is often important to establish what a person knows. If a person buys land but does not know about an interest  (see #15) someone has in the land, can the buyer ignore their interest? To put it another way, are they **a buyer with notice** or **a buyer without notice** of this person's interest, where *notice* means *knowledge*?

There are different types of notice:

1. **Actual notice**. A person has actual notice if they were directly told and received the information. Suppose person A has a right of way over land that person B proposes to buy. If A goes to see B and tells B that he has

been using the right of way over the land, then B has actual knowledge because A told him directly. This is also called **direct notice**.

2. **Constructive notice** (see #74). A person has constructive notice if a reasonable person would have enquired about relevant facts. Suppose there was a gate in the fence that separated A's land from the field that B wanted to buy, and a well-worn path led from the gate across the field to a public road. If B had looked at the field before buying it, they would have seen the gate and the track, and they would have known about a potential right of way over the land. However, B did not visit the field or learn about the track. A court would say that B had constructive notice because any reasonable person would look at a piece of land before buying it. This is also called **implied notice**, **indirect notice** or **presumed notice**.

3. **Imputed notice**. A person has imputed notice (B is treated as if he had actual notice) where A told B's lawyer, even if the lawyer did not tell B. Lawyers have a duty to inform their client about material facts, so the law assumes the client was told.

4. **No notice**. If none of the above categories apply, a person has no notice. So B would be **a buyer for value without notice** (where value means money or other valuable consideration and *notice* means *knowledge*).

In court, **judicial notice** is part of the law of evidence that allows facts to be admitted into evidence (#25) if that fact is so well known that it cannot reasonably be doubted and does not need to be proved. Such facts are admitted under judicial notice and accepted without being introduced by a witness. Examples are the day of the week on which a particular date falls, or that it was dark in England at 11:30 pm because that time was after sunset. In one case in England in the 1960s, the judge was able **to take judicial**

**notice** of the fact that The Beatles were a pop group because they were the biggest group in the world at the time and everyone knew who they were.

## SUMMARY

A notice gives information, requests that we take notice of some information, or gives an order. To lawyers, *notice* is not external but internal. It is in the mind because *notice* is *knowledge*.

# WORD #48: ASSIGNMENT

## Type: noun    Category: land and property

## ITS MOST COMMON MEANING:

1. Setting someone a task

## ITS USE BY LAWYERS:

4. The transfer of a right or a benefit

When I hear the word *assignment*, I am immediately taken back to my school days, when the teacher handed out an assignment, and a deadline was given for when it had to be handed in. It was marked and graded, and then another assignment was set.

More generally, an assignment is a task that is given to someone to complete.

> *Jill's assignment in Canada was to visit all the company's offices to check for health and safety measures.*

Jill has been **given an assignment**, or **sent on assignment**. Her task has been **assigned** to her.

To a lawyer, an assignment transfers something from one person to another. **Assignment** is a legal term whereby an individual, the **assignor**, transfers rights, property, or other benefits to another, known as the **assignee**. This is used in both contract and property law.   The term can refer to either the act of transfer, or the rights, property or benefits being transferred.

Example 1. Suppose A owes $1000 to C. B wants to buy A's car for $1000. A may **assign** the benefit of the contract (that is, receipt of $1,000) to C. B pays C $1,000, and the debt is cancelled.

Example 2. X granted a 99-year lease of land to Y. After 15 years, Y wants to give up the lease, and Z is willing to take over the remaining 84 years. Y assigns the lease to Z. X agrees to the assignment and enters into a licence to assign. X, Y, and Z are all made parties to the licence.

## SUMMARY

In everyday English, an assignment is a task that is given to someone. In legal English, an assignment is the transfer of a right or an interest to someone.

# WORD #49: SUMMARY
## Type: noun    Category: court procedure

## ITS MOST COMMON MEANING:
1. A brief account giving the main points of something

## ITS USE BY LAWYERS:
4. A simplified court procedure

A summary is a shortened version of the full book, article or story. It covers the main contents of the complete version but in a condensed form. Here is a summary of the Shakespeare play *Romeo and Juliet* in 29 words:

> *A tragic tale of two young lovers from feuding families in Verona. Despite their forbidden love, they secretly marry. Miscommunication leads to their untimely deaths, ultimately reconciling their families.*

Lawyers use the word *summary* to refer to a simplified process that does not follow longer or more complex procedures. Take, for instance, the criminal process. A person committed an offence of theft and wants to plead not guilty and have a jury trial. The case is delayed until lawyers are briefed and the case is ready for trial, which can be months or even years later. Trial by jury is a lengthier and more complex process.

Compare that with someone who committed the same offence; they are arrested and brought before the court the next day. If the offender agrees, the court may deal with them on that day, they may plead guilty, and they are sentenced—all within the space of 24 hours. That is an example of **summary justice**, where someone has a **summary hearing**. A court that deals with offenders this way is a **summary court,** also known as a **court of summary jurisdiction**.

The same process may be applied in civil cases. Suppose that the dispute between the parties was the amount owed by the defendant to the claimant for the sale of a car. The defendant said he owed only $2,500, but the claimant produced an email in which the defendant agreed to pay $3,500 for the car. The claimant could apply to the court for **summary judgment** for the full amount. The application could be granted if it was clear that the defence to the claim had no chance of success after a full trial because the defendant clearly agreed to pay the full amount.

Similarly, if a claim for costs is made at the end of a civil trial, a **summary assessment of costs** may be made if the judge has all the necessary information and it is simple to assess costs. If not, costs are decided after a detailed assessment.

Courts can deal with cases **summarily**, meaning instantly, speedily, or in a simplified way.

## SUMMARY
A summary is a reduced, shorter version of the original. Summary legal proceedings are speedy, less complex and instant.

## OTHER ENTRIES THAT USE THE WORD *SUMMARY*
#43 motion

# WORD #50: EXECUTE
## Type: verb    Category: contracts

## ITS MOST COMMON MEANING:
1. To put a guilty person to death.

## ITS USE BY LAWYERS:
4. To bring a document into effect.

Charles I, the king of England, Scotland, and Ireland, was executed on Tuesday, 30 January 1649, outside the Banqueting House on Whitehall, London, for the crime of treason.

*Execute* is one of those words that you could say has the opposite meaning when lawyers use it. Poor King Charles was killed for the crime of treason. When a deed (see #56) is executed, the document is not killed, but rather, it starts its life. Execution is the final act that brings it into being.

The dual meaning of execution sometimes has an unintentionally humorous effect as in this part of a letter that is quoted in the case of Melham v Katter [2013] NSWDC 203, [6]

> *'We refer to your letter ... with a proposed contract attached for our client's execution"*

It would be better to write:

> *... for our client to sign*

or,

| *... to be executed by our client*

and then the client doesn't have to worry about being killed!

A deed requires more than just a signature for it to be executed; a deed must be 'signed, sealed and delivered' (see #29). A more modern phrase is 'executed as a deed', a wording intended to bring together all that is required to bring a deed into effect.

Deeds have an **execution clause** at the end of the document indicating where the parties sign, in what capacity they are signing, and who the witness to the signature was, such as this:

> *Executed as a deed by the Cornwall Council whose Common Seal was affixed*
>
> *in the presence of*
>
> *Authorised Officer*
>
>
> *Signed as a deed by Keith Brewer and Christine Frances Brewer*
>
> *in the presence of:*
>
> *Witness name:*

A contract is not a deed, so it is executed when signed. It does not have to be sealed or delivered.

## SUMMARY

In everyday speech, execution means putting someone to death. To a lawyer, execution brings a document to life.

# WORD #51: PRESCRIPTION
## Type: noun    Category: land and property

### ITS MOST COMMON MEANING:
1. A doctor's note for drugs to be supplied to a patient.

### ITS USE BY LAWYERS:
7. The way to obtain rights after use for a fixed period.

Lawyers use the word *prescription* very differently from everyone else. People are given a prescription after a visit to the doctor, and the prescription is taken to a pharmacist who then supplies whatever has been prescribed by the doctor.

Lawyers use the word *prescription* when they refer to rights over land that have been gained by continuous use over a set amount of years.

Please remember that this book is about language rather than law. The details of the relevant law differ from country to country, but there are some common points.

Suppose that your piece of land is next to mine, and without your permission, I have walked across your land to get to my house and garden. I did not use force to access your land, as I used an existing gap in the fence. I have walked freely and openly in the daytime, and I have done so for many, many years. If you were to apply to the court to stop me, I could defend your claim by saying that the right to walk over your land has been **gained by prescription**. Please note that I do not claim to own your land; I have simply gained the right to walk over your land to get to my house. In many countries, this right of way is called an *easement*, and rights of easement can be **gained by prescription** for a right of way, to light, to air and of support, after continuous use for a set period. That period will depend on what has been decided in each country, which can be in the range of 20 to 60 years - **the prescriptive period**. The rights that have been gained are called **prescriptive rights** or **prescriptive easements**.

## SUMMARY

In general use, a prescription enables you to obtain drugs that your doctor advises. In legal use, prescription enables you to obtain rights over someone else's land.

***Not to be confused with 'proscription'***. To proscribe something means to ban, forbid or prohibit something or someone. There is a proscription against driving a car while drunk. It has been proscribed by statute.

# WORD #52: FRUSTRATION
## Type: noun    Category: contracts

## ITS MOST COMMON MEANING:

1. The feeling or emotion of anger and annoyance at being unable to complete or achieve something.

## ITS USE BY LAWYERS:

(-) Something that occurs to prevent compliance with a contractual obligation.

Frustration is an emotion, and a very strong one.

> *My car broke down, and I couldn't make it to the airport on time to catch my flight. Imagine my frustration!*

In the legal world, someone might be pleased when there is frustration! In contract law, frustration is a defence where the claimant applies to the court for an order that the purpose of the contract cannot be carried out. The defendant can sometimes claim that an unforeseen event has made it impossible to do what was promised in the contract. For example, in the English case of *Krell v Henry* (1904), after Queen Victoria died, her son Edward VII was to be crowned king. The defendant rented from the claimant a flat with a balcony overlooking the coronation procession route, and he paid a £25 deposit, with £50 to be paid after the coronation. Edward became unwell, and the coronation was cancelled. The flat owner sued for payment of £50. The court held that the cancellation of the coronation **frustrated the contract** because the basis of the contract was to view the coronation procession, which did not take place. The **frustrating event** was the cancellation of the procession, over which the defendant had no control.

## SUMMARY

How *frustration* is used generally and legally is linked to a situation that doesn't happen, whether missing a flight or a procession being cancelled. The difference is that in common use, *frustration* is meant to express what someone feels. To lawyers, the frustrating event is just a cold, hard fact, but it can have a happy outcome if the defence of frustration is successful and the claimant is released from their obligation to perform the contract.

# WORD #53: COUNSEL

Type: noun    Category: lawyers

## ITS MOST COMMON MEANING:

1. Advice or guidance on behaviour, a decision to be made, a career change, etc.

## ITS USE BY LAWYERS:

4. A barrister (in England and Wales); an attorney (in the US).

In its everyday sense, *counsel* is guidance or advice given to someone, often when the person who needs it has asked for it. Counsel is often serious and formal because it describes the advice necessary for life, such as relationship or career advice. Counsel is also used as a verb.

> *I would counsel you to cut down on the amount of sugar in your diet.*

*Counsel* is a word that lawyers use to refer to other lawyers. It has a different use and meaning on either side of the Atlantic.

In England and Wales, *counsel* is used exclusively for barristers who are specialist court advocates. As a solicitor, I am never referred to as *counsel*. In the US, *counsel* is used for all attorneys, whether they work only in the law office or appear in court.

The plural of *barrister* is *barristers*. The plural of *attorney* is *attorneys*. But the plural of *counsel* is *counsel*.

> *In total, seven counsel were involved in the hearing, one for each of the six defendants and one for the prosecution.*

The English bar (see #23) comprises **leading counsel** (barristers appointed King's Counsel, with the letters KC after their name, or QC when the reigning monarch is The Queen) and **junior counsel**. In court, barristers can be referred to as **counsel for the defence**, **counsel for the prosecution**, or **counsel for the claimant**, depending on whom they represent.

In the US, *counsel* has several related terms.

**Special counsel** is a lawyer appointed to investigate and potentially prosecute a case of suspected wrongdoing for which a conflict of interest may exist (where, for example, a prosecuting attorney may have to investigate their employer).

**General counsel**, also known as the Chief Legal Officer (CLO), **chief counsel** or **corporate counsel**, is the in-house lawyer who reports directly to the CEO on all the legal affairs of the business.

**Of counsel**: an attorney who has a relationship with a law firm but is neither an associate nor partner, who has a close, personal, continuous, and regular relationship with the firm. In large law firms, the title generally denotes a lawyer with the experience of a partner, but who does not carry the same workload or business development responsibilities.

**Opposing counsel** is a way to refer to the lawyer acting for the other side in a court case.

## SUMMARY

In its everyday sense, counsel is not a person but the advice a person gives. In its legal sense, it is a person who gives legal advice.

Not to be confused with *council* - a body of people elected to manage the affairs of a city or a district. In spoken English *counsel* and *council* have an identical sound, and so in England, it is common to pronounce *counsel* as counSELL, with a stress on the second syllable, to make it clear when a lawyer is being referred to.

## OTHER ENTRIES THAT USE THE WORD *COUNSEL*
#1 action, #2 friend, #5 find, #6 call

# WORD #54: CROWN

Type: noun    Category: general law

## ITS MOST COMMON MEANING:

1. An ornamental headdress denoting sovereignty, usually made of gold embedded with precious stones; a crown.

## ITS USE BY LAWYERS:

(-) The authority of the state in the United Kingdom that derives from the office of the reigning monarch; The Crown.

The difference between the two meanings is that a crown is real; it is physical, it can be seen and held. **The Crown**, however, is a symbol, or a representation, of power that comes down from the monarch (currently King Charles III) and empowers all offices of the state: government, the courts, the armed forces, the police and so on. The Crown is a corporation sole (governed by a single person, the reigning monarch), and as an institution, it is the employer of all government officials, the guardian of all foster children (known as **Crown wards**), the owner of all state land (**Crown land**), buildings and equipment (**Crown property**), and the holder of copyright of all government publications (**Crown copyright**).

Prosecutions are brought by the authority of the Crown. The title of a criminal case is *R v Smith*, where R stands for Rex (Latin for King) or Regina (Queen), *v* means versus (or against), and *Smith* is the defendant's name. The main criminal court in England is called the Crown Court, and the royal coat of arms is on the wall above the bench where the judge sits in all crown and magistrates' courts.

*The Crown* is used this way in all fifteen Commonwealth states (including Australia, Canada, and New Zealand), with a combined population of more than 150 million.

## SUMMARY

The Crown Jewels contain two crowns: St Edward's Crown from 1661 and the Imperial State Crown from 1937. However, one crown—the Crown—empowers all of the state's functions.

## OTHER ENTRIES THAT USE THE WORD CROWN

#20 bill, #33 prefer

# WORD #55: CONVEY

## Type: verb    Category: land and property

## ITS MOST COMMON MEANING:
1. To take or carry a person from one place to another by a type of transport (car, bus, train, etc.).

## ITS USE BY LAWYERS:
4. To transfer title to property from one person to another.

In general English, to *convey* people means to move them from one place to another using transport such as a car or train. The type of transport (the car or the train) is also called a *conveyance*. The train at my nearest station can convey me to London, and outside the station is a bus that can convey me to the city centre.

Lawyers use the word *convey* to describe the transfer of an interest in land. To a lawyer, a **conveyance** is not a bus or a train but a document that transfers an interest in land. To convey an interest in land (see #15), the conveyance must be a deed (#56).

Under English law, **conveyancing** (the documentary process of transferring an interest in land) may be undertaken only by a qualified person who is either a practising solicitor (who may be referred to as a **conveyancing solicitor**) or a **licensed conveyancer**.

The **conveyancing process** has three main phases:

1.   Drafting and agreeing the contract deed;

2.  Exchanging contracts, when each party receives a signed copy of the contract. The agreement is binding from that moment; and

3.  Completion of the transfer (#30). That is the moment when the interest in the land has been **conveyed**.

## SUMMARY

When people are conveyed, they are moved from place to place. When land is conveyed, it stays where it is. It is just the land ownership that is moved from person to person.

See also #29 delivery.

### Other entries that use the word convey

#30 completion, #56 deed

# WORD #56: DEED

## Type: noun    Category: land and property

**ITS MOST COMMON MEANING:**
1. An action, an act, something that is done.

ITS USE BY LAWYERS:
4. A legal document.

In everyday use, *deed* means an act or something done, performed or accomplished, usually with intention. It is linked with doing good, an act of kindness or offering help. As a child, I was encouraged to do a good deed daily. Both Christians and Muslims demonstrate their faith through their good deeds.

By contrast, lawyers use the word *deed* to refer to a formal document in writing that is mostly, but not exclusively, related to land. The phrase "signed, sealed and delivered" is borrowed from this binding, legal document and used in everyday speech to indicate something important that is promised and guaranteed. Think of the Stevie Wonder song *Signed, Sealed, Delivered (I'm Yours)*.

A deed is different from a contract in two ways. You can make a verbal contract using spoken words only, but a deed is always an *instrument in writing* (see #37). A contract requires consideration (the price paid for the bargain), but a deed is enforceable by the person receiving its benefit even when they have given no consideration.

A valid deed:

a. must state that it is a deed and executed (#50)) as such,

b. must be signed, and the signature must be witnessed, (it does not need to be sealed), and

c. must be delivered (#29).

Lawyers tend to follow a format when drafting a deed:

a. the description of the deed, or its purpose; the reason why it has been written,

b. a statement of who the parties are,

c. the recitals (#75) - the background information or reasons why the parties are entering into the deed,

d. the witnessing part, which usually starts with the words, "Now this deed witnesses as follows ... "

e. the operative part: the creation of a mortgage, the transfer of land, a covenant to do or not do something.

f. the concluding part "In witness whereof the parties have signed ... ", and finally,

g. the parties' signatures and the witness' signatures.

There is a tendency still to use archaic language such as *parcels* (#60) (the land involved) and *these presents* (#39) (the statements made in the deed), and in this modern age, this should be resisted. Lawyers find comfort in using language that has been used over the centuries, but it does not create anything more binding or understandable, so let's try to be clear and plain in our use of words.

A deed may be used:

- to arrange a debtor's financial affairs with a creditor, called a **deed of arrangement**

- to set out the terms of a trust (#28) (a **trust deed**)

- to gain a tax advantage by paying a set amount over a specified period (a **deed of covenant**)

- to make a gift of something legally binding where no consideration is given by the recipient (a **deed of gift**)

- to change a person's name (a **deed poll**)

Before the land registration system was introduced (where ownership is proven by producing a copy of the register), title to the land was established by producing **title deeds** or **the deeds <u>to</u> my property** (conveyances, mortgages, leases).

## USES OF THE WORD

Parties *enter into* a deed.

Property is conveyed *by* deed (not *by a* deed).

A document is executed *as a* deed.

A deed *takes effect* on delivery.

The type of deed is stated as *a deed of* followed by its subject:

- a deed *of* arrangement

- a deed *of* covenant

- a deed *of* gift

- a deed *of* variation

- a deed *of* trust.

But we don't say **deeds <u>of</u> my property**, but **deeds <u>to</u> my property**.

American lawyers are comfortable to use *deed* as a verb. British lawyers are not.

> *There were several good reasons why the land was **deeded back** to the grantor.*

## SUMMARY

In its general sense, a deed is something, just anything, that a person does with intention. To a lawyer, a deed is just one thing: a formal document. In the past, when executing a deed, a party would touch the seal with a finger and say words such as "I deliver this as my act and deed". The thing done - the deed - was the formal transfer of land., which may be where the word *deed* combines its common and legal meaning.

## OTHER ENTRIES THAT USE THE WORD *DEED*

#27 title, #28 trust, #30 completion, #37 instrument, #39 presents, #50 execute, #55 convey, #58 undertaking, #75 recital

# WORD #57: DEMISE

## Type: verb, noun    Category: land and property

**ITS MOST COMMON MEANING:**

1. Death

**HOW LAWYERS USE THE WORD:**

3. The grant or transfer of a lease (mainly) or other property

All societies have different ways of saying that someone has died. Some ways are polite, or less shocking, ways of saying it without using the word *death* or *dying*.

> *I'm sorry to hear that your brother passed away.*

There are others like *expiry* or *demise*

> *Jane announced the sad demise of her husband John last week.*

Demise is also used in a parallel way to refer to a loss of position or status.

> *After the demise of The Beatles, George Harrison became a well-known songwriter and had many hit records.*

Lawyers use the word *demise* to refer to the grant of a lease of land. A **demise of land** is a lease of land, and the land that has been leased is **the demise** or **the demised land**. *Demise* is both a noun and a verb.

> *The whole farm **was demised to** her children in 1975.*

> *Here is **a copy of the demise** from 1975. It shows the **demise** outlined in red.*

*Demise* means three things:

1.   As a verb, to grant the lease,

2.   As a noun, the document that creates the lease, and

3.   As a noun, the land that was leased.

## SUMMARY

It is possible that the first use of the word *demise* was a legal one, and it meant to send away land or property, which also happened when someone died. In the 16th century, it was applied to the death of a king and the immediate transfer of land and power to his eldest child, and by the 18th century, it became a word to use as a polite alternative to *death*.

# WORD #58: UNDERTAKING

## Type: noun    Category: lawyers

## ITS MOST COMMON MEANING:
1. A business, or a project

## ITS USE BY LAWYERS:
(-) A binding promise given by a lawyer

It is vital to commit to an undertaking because it involves cost, time, and effort.

> *The construction of a bridge linking Denmark and Sweden was a huge undertaking because of its length and the busy sea traffic there.*
>
> *The company plans to expand its streaming library to more than 10,000 premium titles over the next two years, a risky and ambitious undertaking that could make sticking with the service worthwhile for its millions of customers.*

It can also be used to promise to do something, but in general English, there is no consequence if the promise is broken. If a lawyer gives an undertaking, the promise must be carried out, or the lawyer risks being unable to continue to practice.

The **giving and receiving of undertakings** is central to the better functioning of the court system and buying and selling property, to give just two examples. When working on a deed (see #56), I am always asked to give an undertaking to pay the other party's costs, whether or not the deed is completed (#30). This ensures that the other party will engage in the process of negotiating and drafting the deed.

Similarly, when a property with a mortgage is about to be bought and sold, the seller's lawyer gives an undertaking to the lending company that the amount still due on the mortgage will be paid when the sale money has been received. This ensures that the mortgage company will cooperate with the transaction.

When a sale is at the point of exchange of contracts (#30 and #55), there is no need for a physical copy to be released to the lawyers on each side. One lawyer gives the other lawyer an undertaking that this copy of the contract is theirs, and they are holding on to it in safekeeping until it can be given to the other lawyer. This removes all delay that would arise if a contract had to be physically handed over to another lawyer who may not even be in the same city or country.

An undertaking is readily received because there will be serious consequences if the promise is broken. The lawyer's licence to practice law can be taken away, or they may be ordered to pay a considerable sum if the **undertaking is not performed** (or **carried out**).

Once the promise has been carried out in agreement with the undertaking, the lawyer is then **discharged from the undertaking**.

## SUMMARY

In common use, an undertaking is something huge that requires much effort and time to complete. To a lawyer, an undertaking is a solemn and binding promise to do something.

# WORD #59: CHAMBERS

## Type: noun    Category: lawyers

## ITS MOST COMMON MEANING:

1. A large room or a set of rooms in a building

## ITS USE BY LAWYERS:

2. A judge's private room; the office from which barristers work

The word *chamber* is commonly used to refer to many things, from the chamber of the human heart, and the chamber of a gun (in both cases it refers to a small empty space) to a place where local officials meet to discuss business (the council chamber, for instance) and a huge hall such as the House of Commons of the British Government (the lower chamber) where parliament sits to debate its business. Even Harry Potter was involved with a chamber (*Harry Potter and the Chamber of Secrets*)

Lawyers use the word in the plural form, *chambers*, in two distinct ways: where a judge sits to decide court business, and the business location, or offices, of barristers.

Almost all court business is conducted in public because it is of the greatest importance that the public may observe the legal process and because justice must be seen to be open and fair to all parties. Some decisions may safely be made in private, such as a case in which all the parties have put their case in writing so that the judge may make a decision after having read only the case papers. Sometimes, a judge may wish to hear from the parties' lawyers in the judge's retiring room during a trial. In both of these cases, the judge is sitting **in chambers**, which means *in private.* You may sometimes see this called a hearing *in camera*, because *camera* is the Latin word from which *chambers* is derived. It's nothing to do with taking pictures!

For example, look at the following parts of the daily court list for the Supreme Court List for Monday 29 April 2024, for Melbourne, Australia.

> *Associate Justice Efthim*
>
> *In Chambers 10:30*
>
> *In the matter of an application by Brent Leigh Morgan in his capacity as Liquidator of Toorak Centre Property Ltd (In Liquidation) (ACN 153 841 028)*
>
> *Directions Hearing (Virtual Hearing)*

When the global COVID-19 pandemic prevented meetings from being held in public and court cases needed to continue to be heard, courts used computers to hear some cases virtually. This has continued for routine cases such as a directions hearing, in which the judge makes decisions in chambers about how, when, and where trials are prepared and heard.

For an example of use see the Rules of the Supreme Court:

> *RSC ORDER 52 COMMITTAL Rule 2(4) Where an application for permission under this rule is refused by a judge in chambers, the applicant may make a fresh application for such permission to a Divisional Court.*

## BARRISTERS CHAMBERS

In England and Wales, the legal profession is split into two main groups: barristers and solicitors, with legal executives also making an increasingly important contribution. There are more than 17,000 practising barristers who mainly undertake work referred to them by solicitors.

Barristers are probably best known for wearing wigs and gowns and presenting legal arguments in court. Their most important work is acting as advocates in court and providing expert legal opinions on complex areas of law.

Most barristers are self-employed and work in offices known as *chambers*, to which they pay rent to cover the cost of the building and staff. Barristers may work in chambers or at home, but they meet with clients and other lawyers at their place of work—in chambers.

> *Colleton Chambers is the oldest established set of chambers west of Bristol. Established in 1971, chambers now has over 30 members of chambers practising in various areas of law throughout the southwest and nationally.*

## SUMMARY

When used in its singular form, a chamber is a place where important civic functions are carried out. When used in its plural form, *chambers* is the place where judges and barristers carry out important legal functions.

# WORD #60: PARCEL
## Type: noun    Category: land and property

## ITS MOST COMMON MEANING:
1. An item wrapped and ready to post or deliver.

## ITS USE BY LAWYERS:
4. A piece of land bought or sold as a separate unit.

When you think of the word parcel, you can see a large object wrapped in paper, ready to be sent by post or carrier.

To a lawyer, a *parcel* is a piece of land with clearly defined boundaries.  It is land in one person's ownership, no part of which is separated from the rest by intervening land in another's ownership.

*Parcel* can also be used as a verb, where smaller plots are made from a larger plot (**parcelled out**), or one plot is sold separately (**parcelled off**).

## SUMMARY
A parcel is a defined piece of land. It isn't easy to send that through the post!

# WORD #61: UTTER
## Type: verb    Category: criminal law

## ITS MOST COMMON MEANING:
1. To say something, to speak.

## ITS USE BY LAWYERS:
3. To pretend that something is real when it is a forgery or a fake

In general English, the word *utter* is used in two ways. The first way is to use it as an adjective meaning *complete* or *total*, as in

> What you just said makes no sense. It is utter nonsense.

As a verb, it means to say something or to speak out loud.

> *Julius Caesar is famous for uttering these words about defeating Britain: I came, I saw, I conquered.*

In legal terms, uttering has two stages. The first is to create a false document, such as a banknote, a passport, or a driving licence. This is called forgery. The second is to use it as if it were genuine. If a criminal has a bag of £50 notes that he knows to be forged and uses them to buy a car, that is called *uttering*.

A birth certificate is an important document that proves someone's identity. My birth certificate bears a note at the bottom:

> *TO ALTER THIS DOCUMENT OR TO UTTER IT SO ALTERED IS A SERIOUS OFFENCE.*

The offence was created in 1861 and section 36 of the Act is still in force.

## SUMMARY

To a lawyer, uttering is not about speaking but about doing something silently. The false document speaks for itself.

# WORD #62: WILL

## Type: noun    Category: land and property

## ITS MOST COMMON MEANING:
1. The mental power used to control and direct thoughts and actions or a determination to do something despite difficulty or opposition.

## ITS USE BY LAWYERS:
3. A written statement of wishes about the distribution of property after death.

Finishing this book has sometimes been an act of the will, a determination to finish what I started. At first, it was an idea, "I will write a book about how lawyers use common words in uncommon ways". Before it was completed, it was a case of "I *will* finish that book". It was willpower that kept me going. I have loved the challenge, but it has sometimes required the will and determination to finish it and write the best possible book I can for lawyers to understand the odd ways that lawyers use language.

And by sheer coincidence, I paused writing to make a new will, a revised declaration of my intentions to leave my property when I die. It is a statement of what I will (or intend) to happen, just as completing my book was what I will (or intend) to happen. Still, the name *will* has been given to no other document but the declaration of a person's intentions after death regarding who will receive their property.

Lawyers use the word *will* in this unique way.

## SUMMARY

There are many ways to show determination to do something, but for a lawyer, the most important act of will is to write a will.

# WORD #63: INNS

Type: noun     Category: lawyers

## ITS MOST COMMON MEANING:
1. Buildings typically in the countryside providing accommodation, food, and drink, especially for travellers.

## ITS USE BY LAWYERS:
2. The Inns of Court are the professional associations for lawyers.

There is little difference between a business calling itself a pub and an inn, but at its heart, an inn is a building often found in the countryside that provides travellers with food, drink and accommodation. Inns in Europe were possibly first established when the Romans built their system of Roman roads 2,000 years ago.

There are inns in England, Wales, Northern Ireland, the Republic of Ireland, and the USA, but there are also Inns of Court, which are not connected with businesses that sell beer and provide accommodation. Rather, they are run by the legal profession's governing body.

The **Inns of Court in London** are the professional associations for barristers in England and Wales. Gray's Inn, Lincoln's Inn, Inner Temple, and Middle Temple are the four Inns of Court. They have supervisory and disciplinary functions over their members. The Inns also provide libraries, dining facilities and professional accommodation. Each has a church or chapel attached to it and is a self-contained precinct where barristers traditionally train and practise. They date from the 14th century. All hopeful Bar School students must be a member of one of the four Inns and must attend ten 'qualifying sessions', which are formal dinners followed by law-related talks, before being eligible to qualify as a barrister. The Inns have the sole right to call qualified students to the bar (see #23).

The **Honourable Society of King's Inns** is the Inn of Court for the Bar of the Republic of Ireland. Established in 1541, King's Inns is Ireland's oldest school of law and one of Ireland's significant historical environments. The King's Inns award the degree of barrister-at-law which is needed to qualify as a barrister and be called to the bar in Ireland.

The **Northern Ireland Inn,** now the Court Bar of Northern Ireland, is the professional association of barristers for Northern Ireland, with over 600 members.

**American Inns of Court** were created to improve lawyers' and judges' skills, professionalism and ethics. An American Inn of Court is a group of judges, lawyers, and, in some cases, law professors and law students. Each Inn meets approximately monthly to socialise and hold programmes and discussions on ethics, skills, and professionalism. Beginning in the late 1970s, Chief Justice of the United States Warren Burger led a movement to create organisations in the United States inspired by and loosely modelled on the traditional **English Inns of Court**.

## SUMMARY

Inns are open to all people if they need beer, food, or somewhere to sleep. Lawyers' inns are exclusive to particular members of the legal profession and to members of that particular Inn.

## OTHER ENTRIES THAT USE THE WORD *INNS*

#6 call

# WORD #64: VEST

## Type: noun, verb     Category: land and property

### ITS MOST COMMON MEANING:

1. Noun: an undergarment covering the body from the shoulders to the hips, such as an undershirt, a T-shirt, or the part of a suit worn under the jacket.

### ITS USE BY LAWYERS:

5. Verb: to confer or bestow upon a person some right, power, or interest in land.

In this book, I have been careful to describe words of the same type, where both meanings are in the verb, adjective, or noun form. I have included the word *vest* because it is a common word in general English, and confusion can be caused unless it is explained in its legal setting.

In general English, *vest ownership* means a person owns a vest. In property law, **vest ownership** means giving someone an absolute right to a property. For example, when an individual inherits a piece of land, the ownership rights *vest* in them upon the previous owner's death, meaning they now hold those rights completely and fully.

In the legal world, the word *vest* is used as both a verb and a noun. As a verb, **to vest** means to confer or bestow a right, power, or property upon someone. For instance, when we say that rights **vest in** someone, it means that certain rights have been granted, have become secured, and cannot be revoked. It is also used in employment where **vesting** refers to the process by which an employee earns the right to receive full benefits from their employer's pension plan, stock options, or other retirement benefits. These benefits typically **vest over time**, meaning the longer the employee remains with the company, the greater their entitlement. For example, a company might have a policy where employees are **fully vested in** their pension plan after five years of service. This means that after five years, the employee has earned the right to the full benefits of the pension plan, even if they leave the company.

The noun form **vested interest** refers to a personal stake or involvement in a business or property that allows an individual to benefit from it. For example, if someone has a vested interest in a company, they may have made a financial investment or played a significant role in its operations, benefiting from its success.

## SUMMARY

In everyday English *vest ownership* means that a person owns a vest. In legal terms, to *vest ownership* means giving land ownership to someone else.

## OTHER ENTRIES THAT USE THE WORD *VEST*

#37 instrument

# WORD #65: DISTRESS

## Type: noun    Category: general law

## ITS MOST COMMON MEANING:

1. A feeling caused by mental pain, anguish, anxiety or sorrow.

## ITS USE BY LAWYERS:

10. The taking and holding of property as payment for a debt or claim.

This book has two other words for strong emotions that lawyers use differently to their everyday use: relief (see #38, and frustration (#52). And now there's *distress*. Like the other two, in lawyers' hands, the word has nothing to do with feelings. *Distress* is a lawful remedy whereby the property of a person who owes money can be taken and held to force the debtor to pay the money they owe. Sometimes, the goods may be sold and the money is paid to reduce the debt.

Most countries severely limit its use as a self-help remedy (that is, without an order of the court). If it is still available, it is used where a landlord is owed rent. The tenant's property can be taken and sold, and the money raised can be used to reduce the debt.

A court may order distress under a **warrant of distress** if a fine has not been paid to a criminal court, or in a civil court if a person has been awarded payment of a sum owed and it has not been paid.

The person taking the goods is a **distrainor** who may **distrain for** unpaid rent. The action of taking the goods is called **distraint**. Some items are protected from distraint, such as items required for use in employment or education, so that other goods are **distrainable**, or they are called goods that may be **distrained**.

## SUMMARY

Undoubtedly, a person who suffers distress (having their goods taken to enforce a debt) will feel great distress.

# WORD #66: SEVERAL

Type: adjective    Category: general law

## ITS MOST COMMON MEANING:
1. A small number of things.

## ITS USE BY LAWYERS:
4. Separate, treated individually.

We use the word *several* to mean *a small number of things.*

> *I own several dictionaries but many hundreds of novels.*
>
> *I subscribe to several podcasts but my favourite is* The Rest is History.
>
> *I tried several times to get tickets for the game, but I failed every time.*

*Several* indicates a number greater than two or three, but not a large number.

The word comes from an ancient one meaning *separate* and that is how lawyers use the word *several.*

Andre and Bill each received a loan from Charlie at different times and under separate agreements. Andre and Bill have several (individual and separate) liability to Charlie for a debt, which means that Charlie can sue either Andre or Bill for what each owes him. Andre and Bill owe money separately to Charlie, so their liability is several. Charlie can sue Andre and Charlie can sue Bill each for their own debt, but he cannot sue both of them for just one of the debts.

However, there are occasions when liability is both **joint and several**, where a group of people are liable either together, or separately and singly.

In a contract, joint and several liability arises when two or more persons jointly promise in the same contract to do the same thing but also separately promise to do the same thing. For example, if Andre and Bill promise jointly and severally to pay £100 to Charlie, they are obligated to pay £100 to Charlie. Still, they are also individually under an obligation to pay him the money. Payment by Andre or Bill discharges the obligation. In such a case, Charlie is entitled to £100 in total and the court can enforce the obligation in full against Andre or Bill or both.

## SUMMARY

This is another word that lawyers use in the opposite way to everyone else. In common speech, *several* means a small number, but to a lawyer, *several* means an individual—just one.

# WORD #67: ACCESSORY

## Type: noun    Category: criminal law

## ITS MOST COMMON MEANING:
1. Something that belongs to or is part of another main thing

## ITS USE BY LAWYERS:
3. A person who is not present at the crime but assists before or after it.

> *She wore a green wool suit with matching accessories - shoes, hat, and handbag.*
>
> *The price of the car includes accessories worth over $1,500.*

An accessory is an object or device that is not essential in itself but adds to the beauty, convenience, or effectiveness of something else. On the Apple website, you can see many types of accessories for the iPhone: cases, earphones, and speakers. The phone works perfectly well without them, but they all improve the user's experience of the phone in some way.

In law, an accessory assists a person who commits or has committed a crime. An accessory is not involved directly in the commission of the offence. They may assist before the crime is committed (for example, giving someone a gun or plans of the bank) or afterwards (hiding the offender to prevent arrest). In American law, this is called an **accessory before the fact** and an **accessory after the fact**.

## SUMMARY

In everyday use, an accessory is a thing, an object (but never a person) that improves appearance or usefulness. In law, an accessory is always a person who helps an offender.

# WORD #68: USER

## Type: noun    Category: land and property

**ITS MOST COMMON MEANING:**

1. A person who uses something, like a road user, or phone user.

**ITS USE BY LAWYERS:**

4. The actual and continued exercise or enjoyment of any right or property.

Here's a staggering piece of information. The iPhone was introduced in 2007, and as of 2023, there are an estimated 1.46 billion active iPhone *users* worldwide. That's an awful lot of people at any one time using their smartphone to check emails, send messages and make calls. This means that around 18% of the world's population are iPhone *users*.

In everyday English, a *user* is a *person*. In legal English, *user* is the use of something, not the thing that is used or the person making use of something.

For example, when we looked at word #51 *prescription*, we saw that the lawful right of way over land that you do not own arises over time, and this could be twenty years' *user*, meaning the actual and continued exercise or enjoyment of a right of way for twenty years.

Summary

In general English, *user* is the person who exercises a right. In legal English, user is the exercise of that right.

# WORD #69: BUNDLE
Type: noun    Category: court procedure

## ITS MOST COMMON MEANING:
1. Several things or a quantity of material wrapped or tied together.

## ITS USE BY LAWYERS:
9. An agreed file of papers prepared for, and referred to, during a court case.

In everyday language, "bundle" refers to a collection of items, such as a bundle of sticks tied together, a bundle of clothes to be taken to a charity shop, or a bundle of TV channels offered at a discount. The everyday use of "bundle" conveys the idea of gathering multiple items into one cohesive unit for convenience, efficiency, or value. For example, telecommunications companies might offer customers a bundle of internet, phone, and TV services at a single rate, making it simpler and more cost-effective than purchasing each service separately.

Creating a **court bundle** is a careful and deliberate exercise for lawyers. When a case goes to a hearing or to appeal, there will always be many documents that the lawyers want the judge to read and consider when reaching a decision. The lawyers must always agree upon the documents, both as to their relevance to the case and the admissibility of their content. Once agreed upon, they are placed into categories (statutes, cases, letters, emails, documents, and so on) and then given page numbers and an index. This makes it easier to refer to in court.

> *Your honour, you will find the email dated 8 January 2018 at page 412 of the bundle.*

Or a witness can be referred to a document, and they may find it very quickly while giving evidence.

> *Are you the author of the letter to the bank found at page 227 of the bundle?*

Bundles are sent to the court before the hearing so that the judge may read them in advance, and sometimes, the documents that the parties consider essential reading are separately marked or indexed, with a time estimate of reading them.

## SUMMARY

In daily life, you can bundle anything together, but ask a lawyer what a bundle is, and they will always say a file of papers prepared for a court hearing.

# WORD #70: CAUTION
## Type: noun    Category: criminal law

### ITS MOST COMMON MEANING:

1. Care taken when faced with danger to avoid risk or harm.

### ITS USE BY LAWYERS:

3. A formal warning given to a person suspected of committing an offence that they do not have to say anything.
4. A formal warning given as an alternative to prosecution for minor offences. Also, (-) A notice on the Land Registry.

> *The road ahead is narrow and steep: please drive with great caution.*
>
> *Use caution when picking wild mushrooms as many are poisonous.*

We advise someone to use caution in the same way that we would ask someone to take great care. Some dangers can be avoided if you know the risks and take action to prevent harm.

However, caution has a different meaning for a lawyer. Let us imagine a young person is suspected of committing a minor assault. When arrested, the suspect must be **given a caution**:

> *You do not have to say anything. But it may harm your defence if you do not mention when questioned something which you later rely on in court. Anything you do say may be given in evidence.*

In the US, this is the same as being given their *Miranda* rights

> *You have the right to remain silent. Anything you say can and will be used against you in a court of law. You have the right to speak to an attorney, and to have an attorney present during any questioning.*

**Giving a caution** means telling the suspect that they have the right to say nothing when questioned about the offence they are accused of committing. *Caution* may also be used as a verb:

> *I **cautioned the suspect** at 23:30 before placing him in the police car.*

Let us further imagine that the young person admits that he did commit the assault, but he has never been in trouble with the police before and he had said to the victim that he is truly sorry. The police may decide not to prosecute but instead to **administer a caution** for the offence of assault. It is not a criminal conviction, but it is considered when deciding whether to prosecute a person charged with a later criminal offence.

Cautions are also given concerning land. In the UK, the government holds a register of land which gives details of who owns land and who may have an interest in that land, such as a mortgagee or a lessee. If someone owns land that is not yet registered, they may **enter a caution** that would prevent someone else from registering the land. This is also called **a caution against first registration**. The person entering the caution is called a **cautioner**.

## SUMMARY

In daily life, caution is used if there is a risk of danger or harm. In the legal world, caution is not used; it is *given* by one person to another.

# WORD #71: CAPACITY
## Type: noun    Category: general law

## ITS MOST COMMON MEANING:
1. The ability of something to hold, contain, or absorb, and the maximum amount so held.

## ITS USE BY LAWYERS:
11. Ability or power to act with legal capability.

Last Saturday, I went with some friends to watch a rugby match. I drove my car (the engine's capacity is 2 litres). I filled her up with diesel (it has a 75-litre capacity tank), and the car was full (5-seat capacity). The stadium was at its maximum capacity of 50,000 people, reaching capacity for the first time that season.

Lawyers use the word *capacity* to assess whether someone has the legal power to do something. Right now, I am a fit, sane and healthy adult, and no one would question my ability to hire a car, buy a mobile phone or book a holiday (my **capacity to contract**), but suppose I had too much to drink at lunchtime and I could barely walk or speak. I have suddenly lost my **legal capacity** to enter into a binding contract with these same businesses. My drunkenness might also remove my **criminal capacity** to commit certain offences - mainly those that require specific intention. This could give me a **capacity defence** to a charge of theft or assault with the intention of causing severe harm.

A child has the capacity to enter into a contract for their basic needs (food, clothes). A mentally unwell person may lack the capacity to contract (**diminished capacity**) and the ability to write a will (**testamentary capacity**). That is why it is common for a will to start with the phrase, "I am of sound mind and body," to make it clear that the person has the capacity to make a valid will.

## SUMMARY

The capacity of a petrol tank, a stadium, and a bottle can be measured accurately. But legal capacity is not about size; it is about a person's ability to act in a legally binding way. Legal *capacity* has the same meaning as legal *capability*.

## OTHER ENTRIES THAT USE THE WORD CAPACITY

#50 execute, #59 chambers, #75 recital

# WORD #72: PRECEDENT
Type: noun    Category: court procedure

## ITS MOST COMMON MEANING:
1. An act in the past that may be used as an example to help influence the outcome of a similar act in the future.

## ITS USE BY LAWYERS:
2. A judgment or decision of a court which is binding on (must be followed by) all lower courts.

In everyday language, the word *precedent* generally means an example or event from the past that serves as a guide for future actions or decisions. People often use *precedent* to talk about situations where a previous occurrence sets a standard or expectation. For instance, if a company decides to give employees an extra day off after a big, successful project, that action might set a precedent for similar rewards in the future. The everyday use of *precedent* suggests something that has happened before and can be used as a model or justification for what comes next, but the company might decide not to do that again.

In the legal world, precedent has a much more specific and significant meaning. A legal precedent is a previous court decision that serves as a rule or direction to be followed or applied in future cases with similar issues or facts. The **doctrine of precedent** is a fundamental part of the common law system, where past judicial decisions must be followed by courts to ensure consistency and predictability in decision-making. When a court makes a decision, it always looks to see if precedents have been set by higher courts to determine the appropriate outcome. This practice is known as *stare decisis*, which means *to stand by things already decided*.

When a court decides a case, it considers the relevant facts and applies the relevant law. The central decision is called the *ratio decidendi*, which means the reason for the decision. That key part, the *ratio*, is binding on lower courts.

Legal precedent ensures that similar cases are treated similarly, promoting fairness and predictability in the legal system. For example, if a higher court has ruled that a particular action constitutes a breach of contract, lower courts are generally bound to follow that ruling in similar cases, unless the case can be distinguished in some way. That is a lawyer's skill - to persuade the court to decide either according to precedent, or that the facts are different, so precedent does not apply to their client's case.

## SUMMARY

In everyday language, *precedent* means a past example that guides or influences future behaviour; in legal language, it refers to a past judicial decision that serves as an authoritative rule that must be followed in similar cases in the future.

## OTHER ENTRIES THAT USE THE WORD *PRECEDENT*

#39 presents

# WORD #73: DEVISE
## Type: verb    Category: land and property

## ITS MOST COMMON MEANING:
1. To imagine or plan using careful thought.

## ITS USE BY LAWYERS:
5. To leave property to someone in a will.

It all starts in the mind. If we want to make a plan we devise it: we dream up, think out, think through, think up, come up with, imagine, hatch out, formulate, envisage, scheme, invent, design, fabricate and compose until our thoughts become something real.

> *Our talented engineers have devised a gadget that recharges smartphones using the heat from a campfire. No need for cables and chargers!*

Something else that starts in the mind is the contents of a will, but this is where lawyers use the word *devise* to mean so much more than *to have an idea*. A skilful lawyer will turn the client's intentions into a will, and the deceased's property is then **devised to** the people who benefit from the **devise** - *devise* is also a noun, meaning the will and the property given by the will. A person who is given property by a will is a **devisee**, and the person making the will is a **devisor**.

For centuries, lawyers used this phrase in a will:

> *I hereby give, devise and bequeath ...*

It was once thought that special words were needed to make the gift of land and other property lawful. *Devise* was used about land, and *bequeath* about money and goods, but here is what one court has said: there is no difference.

> '*Even amongst lawyers, let alone lay people, the subtleties of any historical differences between the words* devise *and* bequeath *have generally been lost to view, and both have been overshadowed by the more general word* give. *Each of the words* give *and* bequeath *is capable of embracing a testamentary gift of real estate.' [Anderson v Dupain [2013] NSWSC 108, [30] (Lindsay J)]*

## SUMMARY

A person can devise (think up) the contents of their will. The property they leave is their **devised property**.

# WORD #74: CONSTRUCTIVE

Type: adjective     Category: general law

## ITS MOST COMMON MEANING

1. Serving a useful, positive or helpful purpose. Helping to improve.

## ITS USE BY LAWYERS

2 and 3. Not actual or real but inferred from or read into the facts. Having deemed legal effect.

I showed the first draft of this book to my friend, another lawyer, and asked for her feedback. Her comments, and also her criticisms, were helpful. No one likes to hear negative comments because criticism can be painful, but it is very helpful when offered with kindness and to improve. It is *constructive*.

It comes from the word construct; to build up, to improve, to make bigger and better.

In contrast, lawyers use *constructive* to mean that something is not real or actual but is implied or inferred from the facts. Take the example of an employee who quits their job. It may look like their own decision to resign. However, suppose you asked the employee why they quit, and you found out that the employee had been verbally attacked by their boss, refused overtime work, and not given a pay rise for five years. In that case, it is a clear case of **constructive dismissal** - a course of action taken by an employer that is harmful to an employee and intended to give the employee no option but to resign. A court would not treat this as a decision to leave their employment voluntarily (for which no compensation might be paid) but rather as unfair or unlawful dismissal. It was not a case of **actual dismissal** (the employee was not told to leave) but of **constructive dismissal** - dismissal is inferred from the behaviour of the employer. The employer's behaviour was intended to force the employee to leave. In the same way, there is **constructive eviction** of a tenant if they leave after being forced out by the unreasonable behaviour of the owner.

The courts also use the idea of **constructive notice** to decide whether, for example, a person was properly served with a document such as a subpoena. The claimant may not be able to prove that there was actual notice of the subpoena (it was not personally served on the witness) but if a copy was posted to his work and home address, and copies were posted through and also pinned to his front door, a court could quite easily decide that the witness had constructive notice of the subpoena. (See #47)

## SUMMARY

In everyday language, *constructive* refers to something helpful, positive, and intended to produce good results or improve a situation. Legally, *constructive* refers to a legal inference or presumption about a situation based on actions, circumstances, or facts, even if it is not explicitly stated or intended. It involves legal doctrines where the law treats a situation as if it were true.

## OTHER ENTRIES THAT USE THE WORD *CONSTRUCTIVE*
#47 notice

# WORD #75: RECITAL
## Type: noun   Category: contracts

## ITS MOST COMMON MEANING:
1. A musical performance by a soloist or small group.

## ITS USE BY LAWYERS:
5. Used in the plural, the preliminary statement in a deed or contract showing the reason for its existence and leading up to and explaining the operative part.

Last week I attended a music recital. A friend of mine played the clarinet, accompanied by a pianist. They played six pieces, and they were so good I am going to attend another recital of theirs next week.

A lawyer's recital is just a list of relevant facts, positioned early on in a deed or contract.

A deed is made up of 5 main parts:

1.   A list of the parties

2.   The recitals; those parts that merely declare facts and do not affect the substance of the transaction. They are inserted to explain the reason for the transaction.

3.   The witnessing part, "Now this deed witnesses as follows"

4.   The operative part, such as the transfer of land and the list of conditions

5.  The testimonium, where the parties sign to show their willingness to be bound by the deed and in what capacity they are signing

For an example of some recitals in a deed, go back to *#41 whereas*. The recitals section starts with the word *Whereas*, and the three points that follow are the recitals, the three relevant facts that explain why the employment contract is being entered into. You will sometimes see this section introduced by the word *Recitals, or Introduction.*

## SUMMARY

A musical recital is a celebration of beautiful music. Lawyers' recitals are a dull statement of relevant facts.

# WORDS IN ALPHABETICAL ORDER

Word #67: accessory

Word #1:   action

Word #25: admit

Word #48: assignment

Word #26: audience

Word #23: bar

Word #46: bench

Word #20: bill

Word #69: bundle

Word #6:   call

Word #71: capacity

Word #14: case

Word #17: cause

Word #70: caution

Word #59: chambers

Word #40: complaint

Word #30: completion

Word #32: construction

Word #74: constructive

Word #55: convey

Word #53: counsel

Word #54: crown

Word #56: deed

Word #29: delivery

Word #57: demise

Word #51: prescription

Word #39: presents

Word #42: proceed

Word #10: provide

Word #3:　real

Word #75: recital

Word #38: relief

Word #35: sentence

Word #13: service

Word #66: several

Word #4:　stay

Word #31: suit

Word #49: summary

Word #12: taxation

Word #19: term

Word #27: title

Word #28: trust

Word #58: undertaking

Word #61: utter

Word #68: user

Word #64: vest

Word #41: whereas

Word #62: will

# WORDS IN ORDER OF CATEGORY

## CATEGORY - GENERAL LAW

Word #20: bill

Word #71: capacity

Word #32: construction

Word #74: constructive

Word #54: crown

Word #22: determine

Word #65: distress

Word #37: instrument

Word #34: issue

Word #21: natural

Word #47: notice

Word #9:   person

Word #66: several

Word #19: term

## CATEGORY - LAWYER

Word #6:   call

Word #59: chambers

Word #53: counsel

Word #63: inns

Word #16: practice

Word #58: undertaking

## CATEGORY - LAND AND PROPERTY

Word #48: assignment

Word #30: completion

Word #55: convey

Word #56: deed

Word #29: delivery

Word #57: demise

Word #73: devise

Word #36: fee

Word #15: interest

Word #60: parcel

Word #51: prescription

Word #3:   real

Word #27: title

Word #28: trust

Word #68: user

Word #64: vest

Word #62: will

## CATEGORY - CRIMINAL LAW

Word #67: accessory

Word #70: caution

Word #33: prefer

Word #61: utter

## CATEGORY - COURT PROCEDURES

Word #1:   action

Word #25: admit

Word #26: audience

Word #23: bar

Word #46: bench

Word #69: bundle

Word #14: case

Word #17: cause

Word #40: complaint

Word #24: discovery

Word #5:　find

Word #2:　friend

Word #7:　hear

Word #8:　hold

Word #11: information

Word #45: instance

Word #18: matter

Word #43: motion

Word #44: move

Word #72: precedent

Word #42: proceed

Word #38: relief

Word #35: sentence

Word #13: service

Word #4:　stay

Word #31: suit

Word #49: summary

Word #12: taxation

## CATEGORY - CONTRACTS

Word #50: execute

Word #52: frustration

Word #39: presents

Word #10: provide

Word #75: recital

Word #41: whereas

# ABOUT THE AUTHOR

Graham Gover studied law at Brunel University in West London and qualified as a solicitor in 1983. In the following forty years, he has practised as a legal advisor to the magistrates' court, a police and Crown prosecutor, and a private practice lawyer specialising in building development and town planning.

He established his teaching practice, Second Language Legal English, in 2023 after qualifying as a teacher of English as a Second Language.

Printed in Great Britain
by Amazon